THE PREHISTORY OF SADDLEWORTH & ADJACENT AREAS

W. P. B. STONEHOUSE

Edited by David Chadderton

Saddleworth Archaeological Trust

Published by Saddleworth Archaeological Trust

ISBN: 0-9540702-1-6

Cover Illustation: Bronze Age flint dagger found at Ragstone, above Denshaw, in 1924.

Supported by the
Heritage Lottery Fund

Printed by The Commercial Centre Ltd
Clowes Street, Hollinwood, Oldham, Lancashire OL9 7LY ~ Tel: 0161 681 5014

CONTENTS

ILLUSTRATIONS

COLOUR PLATES

Front Cover

The Bronze Age flint dagger, found in 1924 in three pieces by Norman Gartside, a 12 year old schoolboy, at Ragstone, above Denshaw, Saddleworth (1.5 times full size). Now held in Saddleworth Museum. (Photograph: Barbara Booth).

Plates on pages 53 to 56

TABLES

EDITOR'S INTRODUCTION

The original text of this book was written by Dr. Pat Stonehouse prior to 1995, after suggestions had been made that he should write a summary of his lifetime's interest in the Prehistory of Saddleworth. The unfinished draft was put on a computer disc by Saddleworth Historical Society with a view that when completed it could be considered as a possible future Saddleworth Festival Book. In May 1995, I became aware that help was needed and undertook to assist Dr. Stonehouse to revise and augment the text and to find suitable illustrations.

Later that year the Saddleworth Archaeological Trust was formed with the object 'To promote and publish original archaeological research'. Although the Trust had some funds, it was realised that to print even one book, considerably more money would be needed.

In October 1995, Pat asked that the Saddleworth Archaeological Trust take over the publishing of the book on his behalf, and during the period of Pat's illness up to his death in November 1998, I worked with him on a weekly or so basis, revising his document on *The Prehistory of Saddleworth*, line by line. Pat was able to rewrite and dictate corrections to all the sections, and these were typed into the master copy, which was now in Microsoft 'Word' format. At the same time the references were checked and added to, and a start was made on looking for illustrations to accompany the text.

In the meantime, Ken Booth and I, as Trustees, were investigating sources for funding of both *The Prehistory of Saddleworth* and another book, *Roman Saddleworth*, which Ken had also been preparing for many years. Consideration was also given for funding the completed books by asking for advanced orders.

As Pat's illness progressed, he asked T. G. Manby, former curator of the Doncaster Museum and Art Gallery, a highly regarded archaeologist with special knowledge of the prehistory of the Central Pennines and now the editor of the Prehistory Research Section Bulletin of the Yorkshire Archaeological Society, if he would check over the text of *Prehistory*, to make any corrections and to suggest revisions and additions. Mr. Manby kindly did this; the first set of corrections was typed into the master disc by April 1999 and several more paragraphs and drawings, sent by post, were added during 1999, 2000 and 2001.

In the months before his death in November 1998, Pat arranged for me to take his lifetime's collection of over 10,000 worked flints to John Rumsby, Collections Manager at The Tolson Memorial Museum, Huddersfield. Pat's collection, which had been carefully indexed, was accompanied by his notebooks, in which every find had been meticulously recorded, together with other boxes of maps and notes. Pat's collection (Accession Number 1997.28) now adds to the existing fine collection of prehistoric material that the Tolson Memorial Museum already holds.

During 2000/1, I carried out a number of revisions to the text of the book and I sought and obtained permission from various authors and copyright holders to copy the drawings that Pat had requested for reproduction in the book. Ken and Barbara Booth gave valuable help with this work and Ken also wrote a number of additional paragraphs for the book. Also, at Terry Manby's suggestion, the title was changed to *The Prehistory of Saddleworth and Adjacent Areas*, as Pat himself comments in the first page of the book that the prehistory of such a small area as Saddleworth can not be understood without taking into account that of its neighbours.

In October 2000, we were alerted to the possibility of a Heritage Lottery Grant that might be awarded for publication of works on local archaeology. The appropriate application forms were obtained, and with the help of Oldham Metropolitan Borough Council, the application was duly made by The Saddleworth Archaeological Trust. The request was for financial assistance for the publication and promulgation of two books, *The Prehistory of Saddleworth and Adjacent Areas* and *Roman Saddleworth*, the book that had recently been completed by fellow Trustee Ken Booth.

We were delighted to hear in January 2001 that after considering our application, the Heritage Lottery Fund had decided to make an award to the Saddleworth Archaeological Trust. This would make it possible that at long last both books could be published and their contents communicated by means of exhibitions, lectures and by providing copies to libraries, colleges, schools and museums in the district.

I am grateful for the vast amount of help I have been given in the editing of this book, and especially to Ken and Barbara Booth, Terry Manby, Norman Redhead, John Gilks and Professor V. R. Switsur. I hope the book, imperfect though it may be because of Pat's untimely death in 1998, will serve in some way as a memorial to one of the outstanding amateur archaeologists of the Mesolithic period of the Central Pennine region.

Post Scripts

1) It was realised during the writing and editing of Dr. Pat Stonehouse's book that the lists of finds in the various chapters were continually becoming outdated as new artifacts and sites were discovered. Some additional material has been added during the editing process, but the reader should be aware that the lists of finds are not all-inclusive.

2) Some concern had been registered earlier in 2001 by Norman Redhead, Assistant County Archaeologist for Greater Manchester, about Dr. Pat Stonehouse's radiocarbon and calendrical dates in the book. In view of this, Norman sent copies of Table 2 to Professor V. R. Switsur at the Radiocarbon Dating Research Group at Anglia University, Cambridge.

Professor Switsur wrote back in May and again in June 2001, just as the book was going to the printers, giving an explanation of the recent advances with the calibration curve associated with radiocarbon dating and enclosing a revision to Table 2, 'Saddleworth Radiocarbon Dates'. Concurrently, John Gilks had also contacted me with a table of calibrated dates for the archaeological periods discussed in the book, drawn up in the light of recent advances in the work on the radiocarbon calibration curve.

Dr. Pat Stonehouse had indicated quite clearly to me before his death that he did not want the dates in his book altering in any way. With Terry Manby's agreement, I have therefore decided to include both Professor Switsur's letter and John Gilks's contribution in a separate Appendix 2, so that the reader has an interpretation of the latest situation on radiocarbon and calendrical dating.

David Chadderton, August 2001

ACKNOWLEDGEMENTS

The editor apologises if accidentally copyright has been infringed, as in some cases the original source of drawings is not at all clear. The photographs in this book are the copyright of the individual photographers.

Acknowledgement is given with thanks for the following:

To Neil Barrow, Secretary of the Saddleworth Historical Society for the provision of the original disc of Dr Stonehouse's draft 'Prehistory' and to Jim Carr, Chairman of Saddleworth Historical Society, for access to Dr Stonehouse's articles from Saddleworth Historical Society Bulletins,

To Barbara Booth, for providing and preparing for publication the photographs used in the colour pages, on the cover of the book and several black and white illustrations, and also for her advice on editorial matters,

To Ken Booth, for rewriting several sections of the text, many in the Iron Age, at Dr Pat's specific request, and also for making available his extensive knowledge of local archaeological matters, his library and for the identification and the following up of many of the references, artifacts and drawings mentioned by Dr. Stonehouse,

To Stanley Broadbent, Vice Chairman of Saddleworth Historical Society, for drawing an aurochs specially for the book,

To Peter Fox, Oldham Local History Museum, for access to the collections, and for his information on Lottery Fund Applications,

To John A. Gilks, former Curator of Archaeology at the Tolson Memorial Museum, for permission to reproduce his drawings of the Brownhill finds and the Greenfield Axe from his papers, for checking parts of the text, for checking Appendix 1, for providing additonal material together with photographs of Francis Buckley and a copy of the certificate of the latter's mention in despatches, and for his contribution of a section on radiocarbon dating in Appendix 2,

To Terry Manby for reading, editing and revising the text as it stood in 1998, at Dr. Pat Stonehouse's request, and for suggesting and providing additional material and drawings, and also for correcting parts of the text and advising the editor on a number of subjects including sources for drawings, references and copyright holders,

To Margaret O'Brien, for assisting with correcting the French text in Appendix 1, and for proof reading of the completed drafts,

To Lucy Perry, Team Administrator, North West Region, The Heritage Lottery Fund, for her guidance with the application for the Grant, and to the Trustees of the Fund for the award which made the printing of the book possible,

To Norman Redhead, Assistant County Archaeologist and other members of the Greater Manchester Archaeological Unit for assistance with Appendix 2, with other advice on archaeological matters, for permission to use a map from the Greater Manchester Archaeological Unit Journals, and for proof reading the printer's draft of the *Prehistory*,

To Karen Renshaw, Chief Executive's Department, Oldham Metropolitan Borough, for her help and advice on the Heritage Lottery Application,

To Matthew Richardson, Curator of Saddleworth Museum, for access to the collections from which a number of photographs have been produced,

To John Rumsby, Collections Manager, at Tolson Memorial Museum, Kirklees Community History Service, Huddersfield, for his advice, for allowing access to items from the museum collections, for assistance in contacting copyright holders, and for providing photographs and drawings from Museum publications,

To Professor V. R. Switsur of Anglia University for provision of an explanation and the table shown in Appendix 2, giving corrections to Dr. Pat Stonehouse's Table 2: Radiocarbon Dates for Local Sites,

To David Wilson, Head of Geography at Greenhead College, Huddersfield, for writing the paragraphs on soils in Chapter 1.

Permission to reproduce illustrations was kindly granted by:-
Jean Barnes, for a map from *Man and the Changing Landscape*, written by her late husband, Bernard Barnes,
Dr. Christopher Chippindale, Curator for British Collections at the Cambridge University Museum of Archaeology and Anthropology, for a photograph of Francis Buckley,
Emeritus Professor Keith Brannigan, Department of Prehistory and Archaeology, University of Sheffield, for Illustration 8,
Mrs. Clues and the Mossley Civic Society for a drawing of the Luzley axe from *The Story of Mossley*,
J. M. Collinson, Hon. Joint Editor, The Yorkshire Archaeological Society, for drawings from the Yorkshire Archaeological Journals,
Ruth F. Greenwood and Christine Seville for a number of plates copied from Ammon Wrigley's *Saddleworth, its Prehistoric Remains*,
The Lancashire and Cheshire Antiquarian Society for a drawing and a drawing copied from a photograph from the Transactions of the Society,
Alice Locke, Chief Librarian at Tameside Metropolitan Borough Council's Stalybridge Library, for a drawing from *Tameside Before 1066*,
Professor Paul Mellars, Professor of Archaeology and President of Corpus Christi College, Cambridge University, one of the literary executors of the late Sir Grahame Clark, for the drawings of Mesolithic bows and flint tipped arrows from publications written by Sir Grahame Clark,
Andrew Moore, Collections Manager, The Rochdale Museum, for the recent photograph of the Mowroad Torc,
Dr. Michael Nevell, of the Greater Manchester Archaeology Unit, for maps from *Archaeology North West, the Bulletin of the Council for British Archaeology North West*, and also for drawings and material from his book, *Tameside Before 1066.*
The *Oldham Chronicle* for the photograph of Dr. W. P. B. Stonehouse,
Rosemary Pictor for the Certificate of the Despatch mentioning 2nd Lt. F. Buckley,
Dr. A. J. N. W. Prag, Keeper of Archaeology at the Manchester Museum for a photograph of Accession No. 1976.45, as Illustration 24,
Dr. S. Rathmell of the West Yorkshire Archaeological Service, for an aerial photograph of Oldfield Hall, Meltham,
Phyllis Schofield, for drawings by her late husband, Alec Schofield,
Sheila M. Thompson for drawings from the 1974 Castleshaw Excavation Report by her late husband, F. H. Thompson.

David Chadderton
Trustee and Hon. Secretary,
Saddleworth Archaeological Trust.
June 2001.

INTRODUCTION

This account of the Prehistory of Saddleworth and Adjacent Areas is based on the traditional Three Age System in which prehistory[1] is subdivided into a Stone Age, a Bronze Age and an Iron Age, and ends with the arrival in Britain of the Romans in the first century A.D.

The survey extends beyond the bounds of Saddleworth parish, as the prehistory of such a comparatively small area cannot be understood without taking into account that of its neighbours.

These 'Ages' are themselves subdivided and an attempt is made below in Table 1 to give a rough outline of their chronology and nomenclature. It is to be noted that some Middle Stone Age sites in the South of England have been dated as far back as about 8000 b.c. and earlier, but the earliest in the North of England dates from approximately 7600 b.c.

---

[1] *'Prehistory' is usually taken as referring to the period in our history before written records existed.*

Chronology

Table 1: CHRONOLOGY	
Glacial Maximum	16,000 b.c. - 11,000 b.c.
Late Glacial	11,000 b.c - 8,000 b.c.
Middle Stone Age	8,000 b.c. - 3,500 b.c. Possibly starting at a somewhat later date in the North of England
Early	7,600 b.c. - 6,600 b.c. (North of England)
Later	6,600 b.c. - 3,500 b.c.
Neolithic	3,500 b.c. - 1,700 b.c.
Early	3,500 b.c. - ~~1,700~~ b.c. 2,500BC.
Later	2,500 b.c. - 1,700 b.c.
Bronze Age	2,000 b.c. - 600 b.c. (Note overlap)
Early	1,700 b.c. - 1,300 b.c.
Later	1,300 b.c. - 650 b.c.
Iron Age	650 b.c. - 43 A.D.

Chronogical Table: Author's Note
These dates are based on radiocarbon years and are younger than their calendar years. In order to convert them to calendar years it is necessary to 'calibrate' them. The resulting dates are older than the radiocarbon dates, the difference being as much as 500 to 800 years in the third millenium. No really satisfactory method of calibration has been agreed and an additional problem is that at certain periods of time there has been considerable fluctuation in the amount of radiocarbon (carbon-14) in the atmosphere. The result is that at these times the radiocarbon dates are unreliable. One such period unfortunately appears to be centred on 7600 bc.[2]

In the text both calibrated and uncalibrated dates are used: the 'calibrated' dates are shown in capital letters, the radiocarbon years in the lower case. For example, 2000 B.C. is a 'calibrated' (calendrical) date: 2000 b.c. is in radiocarbon years.

Radiocarbon dates are always accompanied by a ± figure alongside the number. This is the standard deviation, a statistical term, and conveys the information that if the second figure is added to the first and then subtracted from the first, there is a 66% chance of the true radio carbon date falling between the two resultant dates. For example, 2000 ±100 b.c. means that there is a 66% probability of the true radio carbon date falling between 2100 b.c. and 1900 b.c. If the standard deviation is doubled there is a 95% chance of the true date falling between 2200 b.c. and 1800 b.c.

[2]*Editor's Note: An Explanation of Radiocarbon Dating appears at the end of this section (on page 20). An interpretation of the latest situation on radiocarbon and calendrical dating, relevant to the above table and table 2 may be found in Appendix 2.*

Topography

Saddleworth is a moorland parish of some 20,000 acres that lies on the western side of the Pennine watershed and within the drainage area of the River Tame, one of the main tributaries of the Mersey. John Aikin described it in his book *A Description of the Country from Thirty to Forty Miles around Manchester* [28] published in 1795, as 'a wild bleak region of which a very small part is under cultivation'. This description is still true today. Although many of the valleys have undergone industrialisation the moors still remain wild and uninhabited, and for this reason parts of Saddleworth and Marsden have been incorporated into the Peak National Park.

The comparatively high altitude (Black Chew Head reaches a height of nearly 1800 feet (542 metres) O.D.[3] and even the lowest part of Saddleworth where the River Tame enters Mossley is 475 feet (145 metres) above sea level) together with its position in the path of the prevalent moisture laden west winds make it a wet and windy place, appreciably colder than the low lying Lancashire-Cheshire plain to the west.

Moreover, the soil, especially of the peat covered high ground is markedly acid with a pH as low as 3.5. The combination of a high altitude, a high rainfall (55 inches/1400 mm a year in some localities), strong winds and a base deficient soil, makes farming difficult and crop raising a risky occupation.

In the 17th, 18th and 19th centuries, all land suitable for farming in the Saddleworth, Marsden and the adjacent parishes was enclosed - the ground broken up with 'hack and graving spade' - all stone was removed in the process and used to build up the dry stone field walls. Any cairns, walls or banks and clearance cairns of the past would have been removed in the course of enclosure and improvement. The same happened in Calderdale and on the eastern Pennine slope, early clearance cairns only surviving in woodland areas - Hagg Wood, Honley. This occurred in the whole of the Central Pennine area, and probably accounts for the lack of outstanding archaeological monuments and sites.

However, 'marginal' areas such as these have their own particular interest, as they serve as sensitive indicators of climatic and social change.

In many lower western parts of Saddleworth deposits of boulder clay and gravels have been left as a result of the activity of the glaciers of the last Ice Age. Stones and boulders ('erratics') were carried considerable distances from outcrops as far away as the Lake District and the south of Scotland (Broomhead *et alia*, 1933) [85].

During the most extreme development of the last Ice Age, the low lying areas of the Lancashire - Cheshire plain and the Irish Sea basin filled with ice fed by glaciers from the neighbouring mountain areas to a height of 1000 ft or more. However, this ice does not appear to have crossed the Pennine Watershed in our area and no erratics are to be found above the 1200 ft contour level. This means that any flint or chert found above this altitude must have been brought there by man, as neither is present in the local rocks.

The soils[4] of Saddleworth and adjacent areas are generally infertile, showing a downslope sequence from blanket peat on the hillsides and plateaux, to acid podsolised Brown Earths on the upper and middle slopes, to Brown Earths and waterlogged gley[5] soils in the valley bottoms.

The variety of rock types and superficial drifts (till, solifluction deposits and alluvium) does not have much effect on the soil type, as both are base poor: it is the volume and acidity of the soil water that is critical in determining the soil type.

The blanket peat began to accumulate in the Sub-Atlantic period, about 2,500 b.p[6], after the Mesolithic people occcupied the region, as indicated by finding their artefacts at the base of the peat or in the soil beneath the peat. It is arguable that the wetter Sub-Atlantic climate stressed the upland deciduous forest, but the Mesolithic people added to the pressure by burning the forest (for hunting) and encouraging grazing. This made the soil even wetter, as the trees transpire up to 80 litres of water a day in summer, allowing the water retaining sphagnum moss and cotton grass to colonise the soil, which finally suffocated the roots of the remaining trees. The roots of the trees are preserved in the acid anaerobic environment at the base of the peat. (See Illustration 4.)

It is worth noting that the Pennines are particularly narrow between Saddleworth and Marsden, with only half a mile of land above the 1000 ft contour. Francis Buckley, of Tunstead House, Greenfield, who was the great authority on the Mesolithic of the North of England in the 1920s, drew attention to this feature of the Pennines, describing Standedge as 'a bridge joining the much wider areas of the Burnley moors to the north with the Derbyshire moors to the south' and attributed the abundance of flints of the Mesolithic period to the presence of this 'bottleneck'.

The relief of the area is shown in Illustration 1 together with some of the features and sites mentioned in the text.

---

[3]*The term 'O.D.' refers to Ordnance Datum: 542 metres O. D. means a height, to the nearest metre, of 542 metres above mean sea level (at Newlyn.)*

[4]*The paragraphs on soils, above, were kindly contributed by David Wilson, Head of the Department of Geography at Greenhead College, Huddersfield.*

[5]*'gley' is a technical term for a waterlogged clay with a blue-grey colour arising from Fe++ ions.*

[6]*'b.p.' (before present) is taken as the date 1950 A.D.*

The terms 'Central Pennines' and 'South Pennines' are both used in this account.

i) The 'Central Pennines' are defined by B. Barnes, 1982, as the Millstone Grit area south of the Aire Gap and north of Longdendale.

ii) The expression 'Southern Pennines' includes all the geologically diverse limestone, coal measures and gritstone uplands area south of the Aire Gap in the Pennines, down to the Trent Basin. (R. Jacobi et al., 1976).

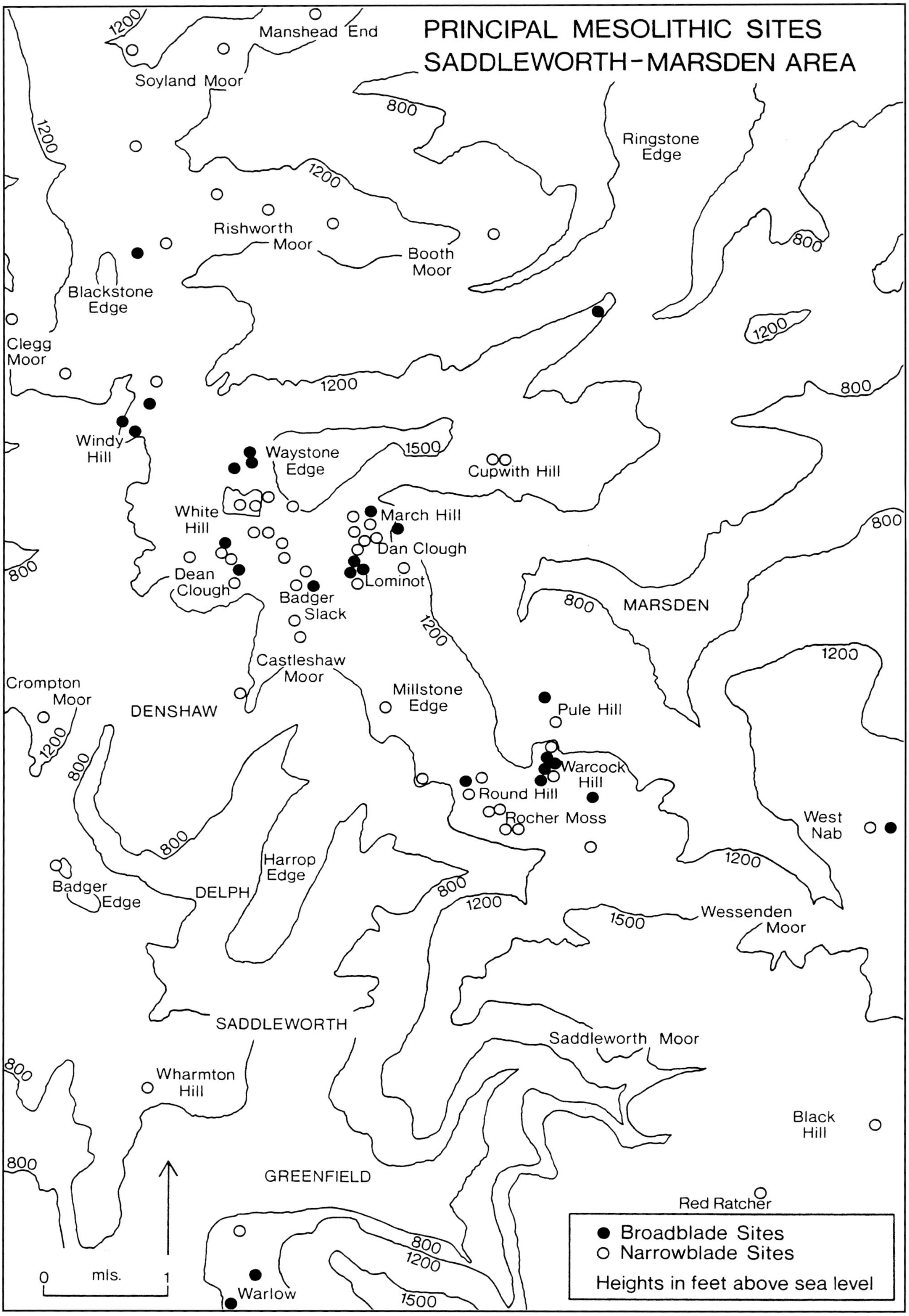

Illustration 1 - Principal Mesolithic sites in the Saddleworth - Marsden Area. (Reproduced from 'Man and the Changing Landscape' by the late Bernard Barnes, by kind permission of Jean Barnes)

Geology

The rocks of which Saddleworth is formed belong to the Millstone Grit and Coal Measure Series of the Carboniferous Period and consist of alternate layers of coarse gritstones, finer sandstones and shales. The sandstones withstand weathering and often stand out as a line of crags, locally called 'Edges', which are split by natural jointing into stacks and chimneys which provide training for rock climbers. The shales form a steep concave slope beneath the overlying edges. The resulting rock scenery is among the most dramatic in the Pennines, vying with that of Kinderscout in the High Peak.

The junction of the porous gritstones and the impervious shales below is marked by a line of springs, where many of the older farmsteads are sited and which would have been attractive to prehistoric man.

The structure of the rock formation is that of an upfold, running north-south with a steep west escarpment and a gentler eastern slope. The dip of the eastern slope is so gentle that in many places it results in the creation of an ill-drained plateau covered with peat which can be as much as 15 feet thick and which is currently undergoing erosion (Broomhead *et alia*, 1933) [85]. It is this erosion which helps to reveal the flint knapping sites left by Middle Stone Age man.

Flint has its origin in chalk formations such as the Yorkshire and Lincolnshire Wolds, some seventy miles to the east: whilst chert (which is very similar to flint) has its origin in limestone. Chert from Ribblesdale can be found in the Burnley area, brought down by the Ribblesdale glacier.

Climatic and Environmental Change

W.G. Hoskins [13] in his famous book *The Making of the English Landscape*, published in 1955, wrote - 'On unpeopled moorland... little or nothing is alien to the natural scene. We see it precisely as the first man saw it'.

A very different view is expressed in a book published in 1982 entitled *Prehistoric and Roman Archaeology of North-East Yorkshire* edited by D.A. Spratt [33]. The North-East Yorkshire moorlands are not dissimilar to the South Pennines, yet in the summary of the chapter on the environment the authors write '...We can be confident when we say that not only are the North-Yorkshire Moors now a man-made landscape but they were certainly so in Roman times and in the Iron and Bronze Ages, becoming so in Neolithic and Late Mesolithic times and possibly changing in that manner in the Earlier Mesolithic and Terminal Palaeolithic'.

Dimbleby (1978) [48], when discussing peat formation in the uplands such as the Pennines, wrote 'I believe we would still have forest if there had not been repeated destruction by fire and grazing from Mesolithic times onwards'.

Illustration 2 - Bare peat moors. The Good Hill Site, with Pule Hill in the background. (Photo: Dr W.P.B.Stonehouse)

Looking across our bare bleak peat covered moors (see Illustration 2) it is difficult to appreciate the startling climatic and environmental changes which have taken place since man returned to Britain as the last Ice Age began to relax its grip. The last glacial period in Britain started some 70,000 years ago and came to its end about 8000 b.c. During most of this time Britain presented an open, tundra like landscape, not unlike that of Northern Canada. The end came rather suddenly and within a few decades (Simmons, I. G.) [86][7], this open landscape, home to herds of reindeer and horse, was replaced by a forested environment, and the reindeer and horse made way for forest animals such as red deer, roe deer, wild cattle and wild pig.

There was, at this Post Glacial time, no barrier to the immigration of either plants or animals from the rest of Europe as sea levels were still very low as a result of so much water being locked up in the great ice sheets, and much of the North Sea and the English Channel was land. The first trees to arrive included birch and willow, to be joined by scots pine. Conditions of climate continued to improve and these species were in due course followed, and indeed dominated by oak, lime, elm, ash, alder and hazel, the trees of temperate woodland.

Tom Woodhead wrote a pioneer paper covering this subject in March 1923 in 'The Naturalist' entitled 'Botanical Survey and Ecology in Yorkshire'. Later, in 1930, The Tolson Memorial Museum issued a Handbook, again written by Tom Woodhead, *Climate, Vegetation and Man in the Huddersfield District* (Tolson Memorial Museum Publication No. 8) [87].

---

[7]Editor's footnote: Simmons, I. G., writes in 'The Environmental Impact of Later Mesolithic Cultures' (1996) 'Evidence from the Greenland ice-cores suggests that some of the major warming took place within decades, rather than centuries.' [86] p.10.

In Mesolithic times, herds of wild deer and wild cattle would be present in the forests, together with the more solitary roe deer and wild pig, and probably in very hot weather herds of wild deer would visit the more open hill tops. During the early autumn season the roar of the rutting red deer stag would be a familiar sound on the Saddleworth hills.

The red deer would probably be much larger than the modern wild deer of the Scottish Highlands and the wild cattle would be of a type now extinct ('aurochs') and much larger than domestic cattle (see Illustration 3).

Carnivores would include the wolf, fox, bear and badger, and beavers may well have created small lakes which would attract water fowl. Hares (but not rabbits) would be abundant and in the very beginning of the Mesolithic may well have been of the species known as the blue hare (*Lepus timidus*), which turn white in winter. The blue hare can still be seen in the district, but this is the result of it having been re-introduced early in the 20th century. Wild swans and wild geese would visit any open stretches of water in winter. In other words, the hills and valleys of Saddleworth and its neighbourhood would have provided an extraordinarily rich hunting environment.

As the final ice sheets continued to melt, sea levels began to rise into the North Sea basin, until by about 6000 b.c. Britain became an island. The continental-type climate, that prevailed after 8000 b.c., with short dry summers and long cold winters, changed to a warmer, wetter one by about 5000 b.c. when the forest reached its climax. Then, about 3000 b.c. (in radiocarbon years) - which is circa 4000 b.c. when 'calibrated' - there was a sudden decline in the elm, which presaged a general reduction in tree cover. This may well have been the result of the activities of the first farmers of the New Stone

Illustration 3 - Aurochs Bos primigenius. A wild ancestor of domestic cattle in Europe. Six feet tall at the shoulder. (Kindly drawn for this publication by Stanley Broadbent.)

Age who needed open land for crop raising and the pasturing of their domestic animals. With the aid of fire and polished stone axes, they made clearings in the forest, cut foliage for cattle fodder, and a more open landscape evolved, especially in limestone and chalk areas with base rich soils of high fertility. This process continued throughout the subsequent Bronze Age and the Iron Age into historic times.

The evidence for the environmental changes sketched above is provided mainly by the study of tree and grass pollens, which in a suitable environment persist and remain identifiable for thousands of years. These pollens rain down on lakes and bogs and dryland to leave stratified evidence of past vegetation. The situation on our moorlands was somewhat different. The land above the 400 metre O.D. contour remained comparatively open and as there does not appear to be any climatic explanation for this, it seems probable that Mesolithic man himself may have kept the high ground open by deliberately and systematically burning the vegetation. The evidence for this is the presence of minute traces of charcoal in almost all the soil 'profiles' examined by pollen experts in the Central Pennines at altitudes above 400 metres.

The object might have been to create suitable hunting areas and to increase the amount of browse available to deer. Moreover, these open areas would encourage the growth of hazel, a light demanding and fire resistant tree, whose nuts provided a valuable source of food to these hunter/gatherers.

At first sight it appears very easy to distinguish between the activities of hunter/gatherers and those of farmers, but Fowler (1983) [34] has pointed out that the sort of activities described above show that man was beginning to manipulate his environment and that 'it is but a short step to herding animals and selectively encouraging floral regeneration, even planting 'strangers', in such clearings'.

Chaplin R.R. (1975) [44] pointed out that 'red deer are social animals whose behaviour could predispose them to manipulation by early man' and Mellars (1975) [45] commented 'How far this pattern of man-animal relationship can be described as a simple form of 'domestication' would seem to reduce largely to a question of the definition of terms'.

Christine T. Williams (1985) [35] during her researches on Soyland Moor near Blackstone Edge, near Littleborough, considered that there had been two long periods of clearance activity which she attributed to grazing pressure. It was claimed there was no direct evidence of fire at this site.

The repeated burning of the vegetation and the destruction of trees may have been factors leading eventually to the development of blanket bog. The presence of trees on the moors in the past is demonstrated by their pollens but more dramatically by finding the actual roots and stumps of trees in the lower levels of the peat (see Illustration 4).

These are usually of birch and pine and must have been preserved by the very rapid development of protective peat.

It seems likely, therefore, that the transition from a wooded, or at least a shrubby landscape on our hills to its present impoverished state was initiated by these small Mesolithic hunting groups, though the change to a wetter and cooler climate may have had some contribution.

Illustration 4 - Roots and stump of a Mesolithic tree found in the lower levels of the peat. (Photograph: Dr. W.P.B. Stonehouse)

Historical Background

In 1871, John Aitken of Bacup and James Binns of Halifax were searching for glacial erratics on the moors and discovered a number of flints. Some of these tools, now known as microliths, were remarkably small and became known as 'pygmy flints', some of which were obviously tools fashioned by prehistoric man. It was believed that the fineness of the workmanship precluded a natural origin.

The type of flint used does not occur locally, and as mentioned previously, it must have been imported by man.

Many others confirmed their findings and R. Law and J. Horsfall 1882 [62] and 1886 [63] pointed out that these distinctive 'pygmies' were always to be found at the base of the peat or in the soil beneath the peat, in contrast to the leaf-shaped arrowheads of the New Stone Age and the barbed and tanged arrowheads of the Bronze Age, which frequently occured within the peat itself. Peat formation had therefore occurred at a date subsequent to the deposition of these 'pygmy' tools.

The names of other workers in this field include those of Dr. Colley-March of Rochdale (who excavated at March Hill), Fred Allen of Greenfield, and Ammon Wrigley, the Saddleworth poet and writer who published an excellent little book in 1911 entitled *Saddleworth - its Prehistoric Remains* [10]. This book gives a good account of these moorland flint sites, but it remained for Francis Buckley of Greenfield to carry out much more extensive and scientific field work, extending from Knowl Hill, near 'Owd Betts' in the north, to Longdendale in the south.

Buckley made drawings of most of his more interesting finds and also carried out a number of excavations and what is more, published some of his findings. His manuscripts and maps are preserved in the Tolson Memorial Museum, Huddersfield and form a sort of treasure trove which modern workers can consult. During the 1920s Francis Buckley was in touch with many of the more eminent French and Belgian archaeologists, including the Abbé Breuil, and he became an acknowledged authority on the British Mesolithic.

Francis Buckley's great achievement was that he recognised the existence of two different industries on our hills, which he named the Broad Blade Industry and the Narrow Blade Industry.

Other useful sources of information are *Early Man in The District of Huddersfield*, Petch, J. A., (1924) [37], where the account of the Mesolithic is based on Francis Buckley's work, and *Early Man in the Halifax District*, Watson, G. G., (1952) [58]. Watson went over much of the same ground as Petch, but took in the Aire-Calder watershed moors.

(An account of Francis Buckley's life and of his work may be found in Appendix 1.)

Grahame Clark, who later became Sir Grahame Clark, Master of Peterhouse, Cambridge, and Disney Professor of Archaeology at Cambridge and one of the great authorities on the Mesolithic Age, visited Francis Buckley at his home, Tunstead House, Greenfield, when he was writing his definitive textbook, *The Mesolithic Age in Britain* [36], published in 1932. He accepted Francis Buckley's flint typology, but used the terms 'Non-Geometric' and 'Geometric' to describe the two industries. However, Buckley's original terminology remains in general use.

It is now recognised that the Middle Stone Age can be subdivided into an Earlier and a Later Mesolithic, which are characterised by the Broad Blade Industry and the Narrow Blade Industry respectively.

The most recent account of Saddleworth's Prehistory is to be found in Bernard Barnes' book, *Man and the Changing Landscape*, published in 1982, [1]. This, however, covers a much wider area, from Boulesworth Hill near Burnley in the north, to Longdendale in the south, but is nonetheless invaluable.

Editor's note: Carbon-14 dating

Carbon-14 is a radioactive isotope formed as a result of the Earth being bombarded with particles from the cosmos. The radioactive carbon-14 forms carbon-14 dioxide, which is photosynthesised by plants into carbohydrates. Hence carbon-14 eventually becomes incorporated into all living things.

Carbon-14 has a half life of 5730 years, i.e. after 5730 years its radioactivity has decayed to half that of when it was formed. The ratio of carbon-14 to carbon-12 (the non radioactive form of carbon) is 1 to 12 million million and this ratio has been more or less constant over long periods of time. Whilst a living organism is alive, the ratio of the two carbon isotopes stays the same, since any carbon-14 that decays is replaced by a fresh intake of the carbon-14 isotope. However when the organism dies, the locked-in carbon 14 starts to decay and the ratio of carbon-14 to carbon-12 changes.

So, if say, a piece of plant charcoal is taken for analysis from an archaeological site and the ratio of carbon-14 to carbon-12 had, for example decayed from 1:12 million million down to 1:24 million million, this would mean that the carbon-14 in the sample would have reached its half life and the charcoal sample could be dated at around 5730 years old. Hence determination of the ratio of carbon-14 to carbon-12 can be used to date an archaeological plant or animal sample.

The accuracy of this dating is discussed by Dr. Pat Stonehouse in the note below Table 1, and modern interpretation may be found in Appendix 2.

CHAPTER ONE

Mesolithic (The Middle Stone Age)

7600 b.c. to 3500 b.c.

Saddleworth's prehistory starts in the Middle Stone Age. There is no evidence that man ever put foot in this part of the world before the end of the last Ice Age (the Late Glacial, after the withdrawal of the main Devensian Ice), apart from a single shouldered point (presumably a projectile head) found on Cupwith Hill, Marsden and illustrated in Petch, 1924 (p.24. fig.6) [37] and a large angle-backed point from Blackstone Edge (E. Derby collection).

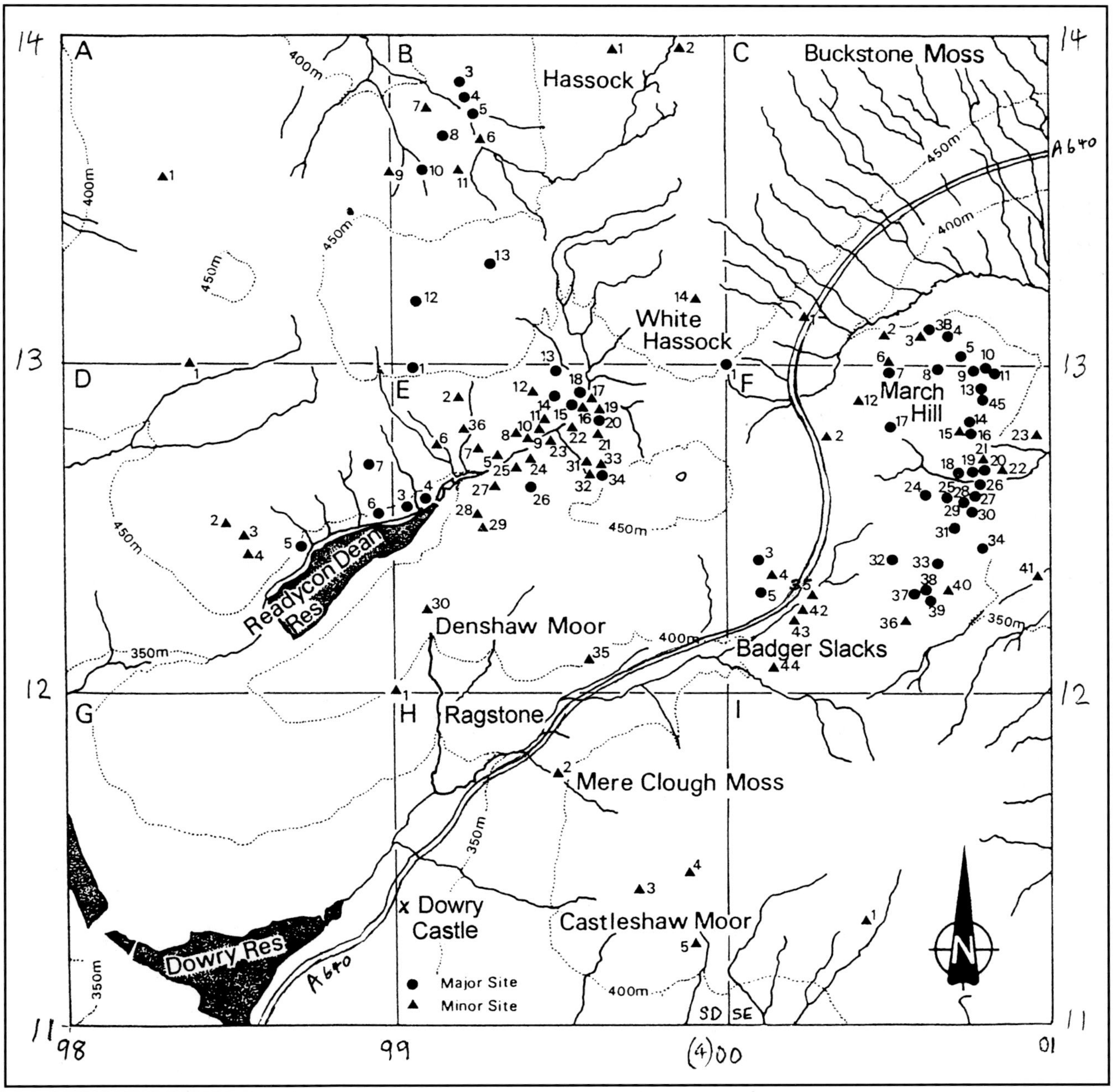

Illustration 5 - Map of Mesolithic sites in a nine sq. kilometre area on the Pennine watershed, west of March Hill. O.S. grid references and the route of the A640 have been added to the original drawing.

(Taken from The G.M.A.U Journal, Vol. 3, p 6, Reference [74], (where the key to the site numbers and descriptions may be found) by kind permission of The Greater Manchester Archaeological Unit).

Similar implements have been found in Derbyshire caves and indeed there is evidence that groups belonging to the latter part of the Ice Age penetrated as far north as the Craven district of Yorkshire and Kirkhead Cave in Furness, Cumbria, so the finding of such a tool in this area need occasion no surprise.

The Middle Stone Age in the Saddleworth-Marsden area has an extraordinarily high density of sites, possibly the highest in Britain. The main local sites are shown in Illustration 1, which is from Bernard Barnes' book, *Man and the Changing Landscape*. The high density is shown in Illustration 5, where a selection of the 111 known sites is shown in one small area of nine square kilometres straddling the Pennine watershed, an area which includes the well-known flint collecting grounds of Dean Clough and Badger Slacks in Saddleworth and March Hill and Lominot just over the boundary in Marsden. A second map (Illustration 6) shows a further area, identical in size and shape, which lies some 5 km to the south-east and which also straddles the Pennine watershed. This is an

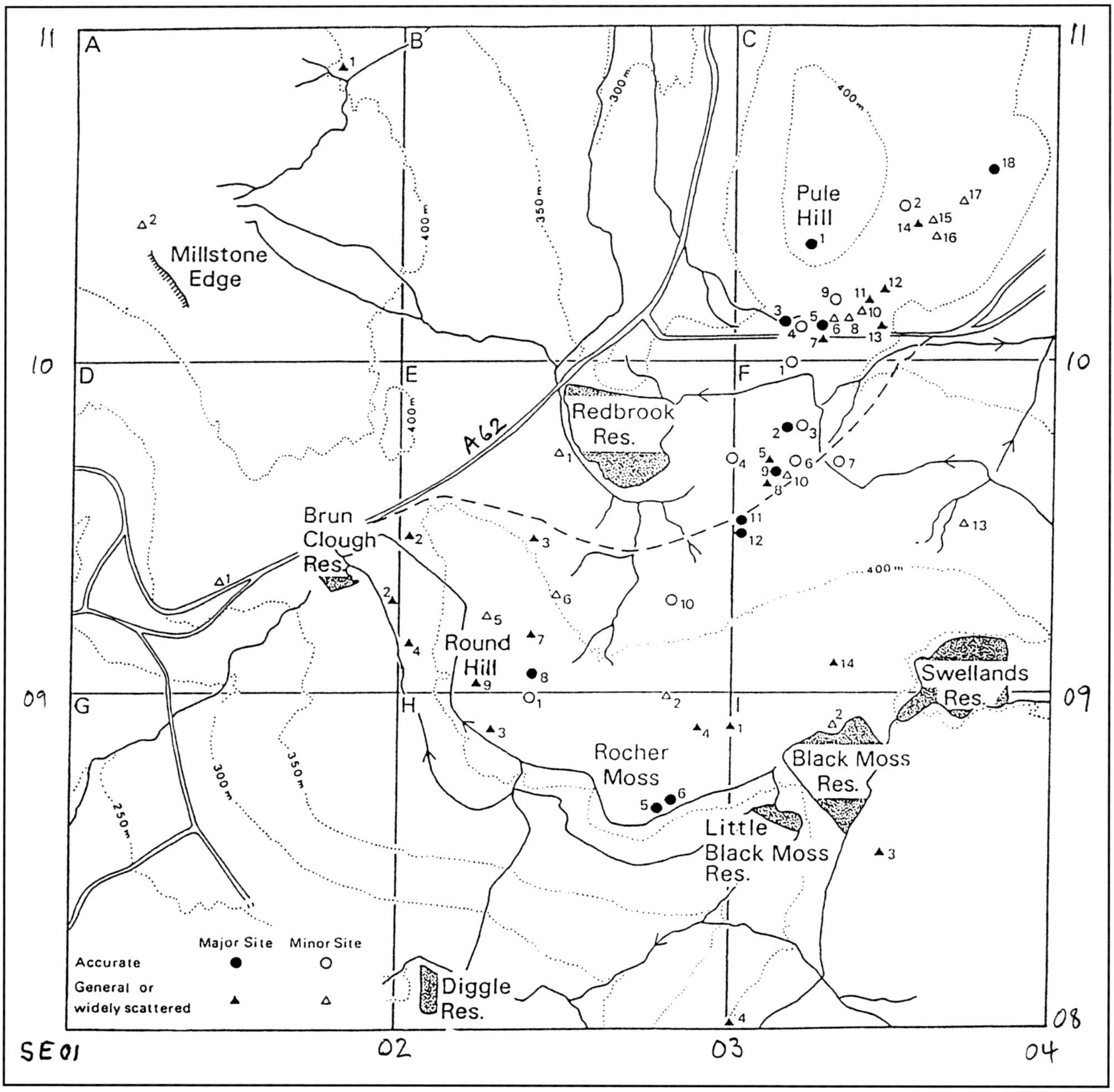

Illustration 6 - Map of Mesolithic sites in a nine sq. kilometre area on the Pennine watershed south west of Pule Hill. O.S. grid references have been added to the original drawing. (Taken from The Bulletin of the C.B.A. North West, No. 8 (Vol. 2, Part II) p. 39, Reference [51], (where the key to the site numbers and descriptions may be found) by kind permission of the C.B.A. North West).

area where the Pennines are at their narrowest, indeed there is only 0.8 km of land of land above 366m (1200 ft.) OD between Diggle and Marsden. This 1200 ft contour line shows clearly on Illustration 1.

Some of these 'sites' refer to the finding of but a single flint, but 40 of them contain a minimum of 150 flints, and the presence of flint debitage shows that these were in fact flint knapping sites - in other words, true occupation sites, occupied for the space of at least a few hours, but more likely several days or even weeks, and usually with evidence that flint knapping had taken place (Stonehouse 1987-88, [74] and 1994) [51].

When these sites are excavated they can be shown to consist of several hundred or even several thousand flints, usually forming an oval shaped scatter, with a sharply demarcated edge. The area covered may vary from 4 square metres to 150 square metres or more. The sharply defined edge suggests the possibility of a hut or windbreak and Francis Buckley (1924) [38] noted that one of his sites at Badger Slacks, which lies close to the A640 road near the Saddleworth/Marsden border, had a 'litter of burnt wood (ling and birch) thickest in a half circle at one end', and added, 'it suggests forcibly a rude shelter made of tree branches'. Stephen Poole 1986 [5] found an arc of small post holes defining a late site at Piethorn Brook near Milnrow.

Nearly every site appears to have had a hearth, a roughly circular area often about one metre in diameter in which most of the flints have been burned, and where there is a concentration of charcoal. One local site, Dan Clough 1, near March Hill, Marsden, excavated by Stephen Poole, revealed an obvious hearth, with a pavement of stone slabs and edged by small upright stones containing charcoal and burnt flints.

Illustration 7 shows the distribution pattern of larger artefacts in an Early Site (Turnpike), together with its probable hearth.

Roger Jacobi has shown that no less than 57% of Mesolithic sites in Northern England lying between an east-west transect running from Driffield to Lancaster in the north and another from Lincoln to Chester in the south, occur in the 5.9% of ground above 1200 feet O.D. and that the density of such sites falls off in a very striking way below the 1200 feet contour (R. M. Jacobi, J. H. Tallis and P. A. Mellors, 1976) [2].

However, agricultural and industrial activities must have destroyed and buried many sites below the 1200 ft contour, and recently field work in the Northern Pennine dales has revealed a series of flint scatters running along the valleys of Weardale, Teesdale, Swaledale, and Wensleydale. (Coggins, T., Laurie, T.C., and Young, R., 1990) [70]. This is in sharp contrast to the situation in the Central Pennines and the North York Moors.

The favourite locations for sites are the summits of gentle hills with widespread views: south facing slopes: near springs and along shelves above streams.

The highest ground is less frequenty utilised, but sites have been found in very exposed situations such as the summits of Pule Hill near Marsden, and of West Nab near Meltham, and flints have even been found on the top of our highest local hill, Black Hill, which is 1900 ft O.D. and near the Holme Moss mast.

Forty eight items of flint were recovered during the excavations of the Roman Forts at Castleshaw in 1984-88. Twenty eight were of Mesolithic Age and had been worked. Again the site is on a south

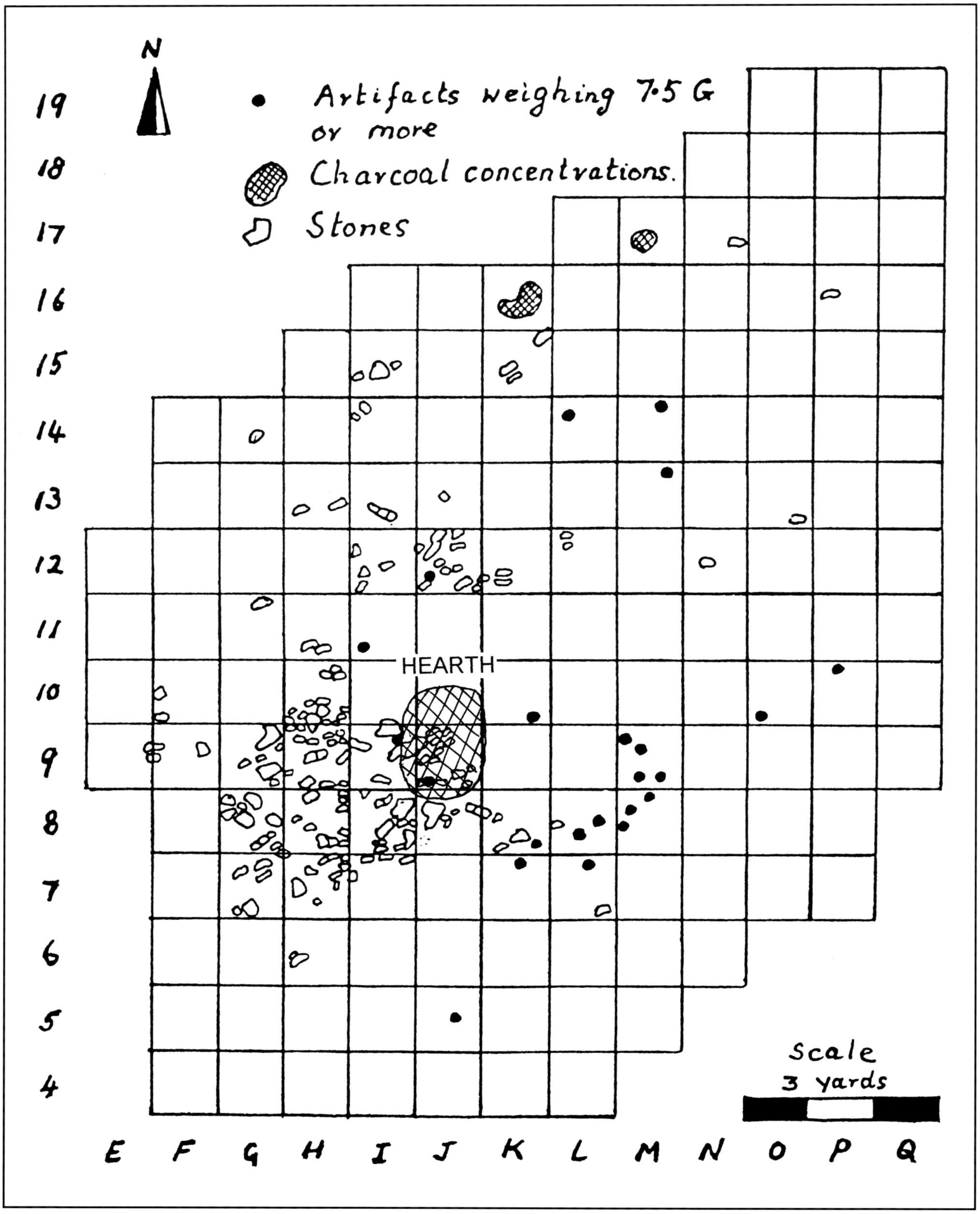

Illustration 7 - Turnpike Site, showing the pattern of larger pieces (> 7.5 gms) from the Early Mesolithic site, together with the probable position of the hearth. (Reproduced from The Yorkshire Archaeological Journal, Vol 64, p. 7, Reference [67], by kind permission of the Hon. Joint Editors of the Y.A.S.)

west facing slope with widespread views. These excavations also produced a Neolithic leaf shaped arrowhead and a Bronze Age barbed and tanged arrowhead (see the Record Cards of the Excavations of Castleshaw Roman Forts, 1984 - 88, Oldham Museum)*.

Sites such as Pule Hill and West Nab might have been used as outlook posts for game crossing the lower ground overlooked by these commanding positions.

An unusual site is that of Pule Hill Bents, which lies on a sloping plateau just outside the Saddleworth Boundary, to the east of Pule Hill. (Stonehouse, 1997) [80]. This produced approximately 100 tools, one of which belongs to the Early Mesolithic Broad Blade Industry, the rest to the Narrow Blade Industry. The great interest is that excavation showed that these tools were unaccompanied by any pieces suggestive of flint knapping on the site. One suggestion is that this was a 'Kill' site where game was ambushed, perhaps over a period of many years. Another possibility is that it may represent the loss of a bag of implements.

Occasionally, a number of tools are found in such a small space that it strongly suggests the loss of a bag of arrowhead points or barbs, or possibly a cache. One example of such a find is at 'White Hassocks', again just outside the Saddleworth boundary, at SD999132 on the moors to the north-east of Denshaw. Here 46 scalene triangles (flint triangles with the three sides of unequal length) were found in $2\frac{1}{2}$ square metres, 40 of which were in a $\frac{1}{4}$ square metre. (Stonehouse, 1978) [57].

Francis Buckley found 33 microliths, (triangles and trapezoids) on the edge of an artificial watercourse on the southern slope of White Hill, which lies on the north side of Dean Clough, not far from Denshaw. They were arranged in a more or less straight line, approximately 2 inches apart and extending for a little less than 2 yards. He considered rather improbably, that they were 'the teeth of some kind of saw' (Oldham Chronicle, Dec. 15th, 1923) [66].

Other suggestions include the idea that the flints might be the lateral barbs of a harpoon, or a device used in some operation analogous to weaving or combing, but the triangles definitely belong to the Mesolithic - and therefore before the days of domestic animals. Altogether the find represents an enigma, although much shorter arrangements of such tools have been found more than once, and do indeed suggest barbs on the side of an arrow shaft.

One recent find, made by Lee Cherry near the head of Heyden Brook, (which runs from Black Hill down to Longdendale) at an altitude of 500 metres, had five triangles, three on one side, two on the other, with a point at the head which looked remarkably like the remains of some sort of barbed arrowshaft or spear, the wooden shaft having perished.

Another example, from Urra Moor, North Yorkshire, is shown in Illustration 8.

** Editor's Note: This paragraph was inserted in 2001 from information provided by Ken Booth.*

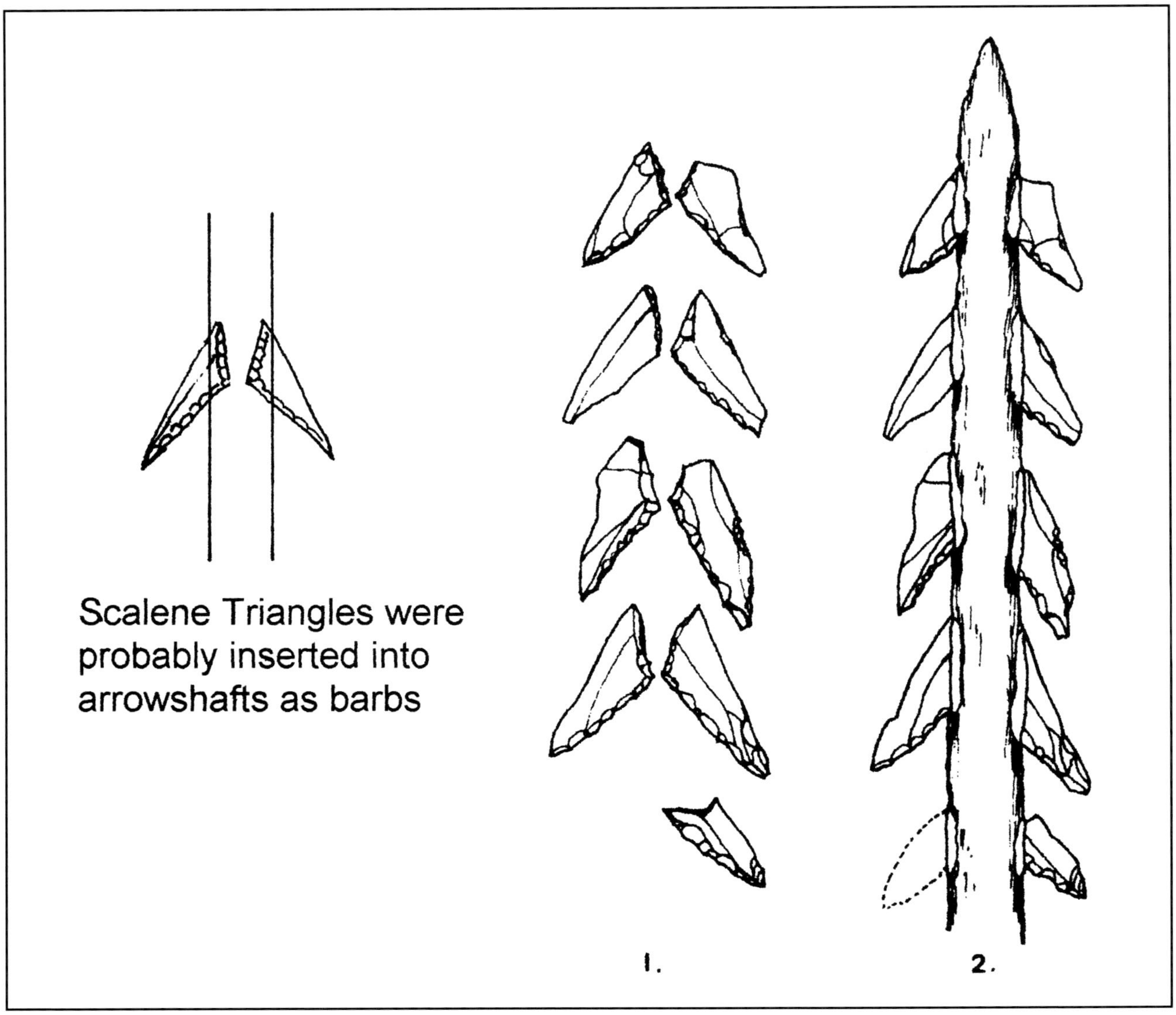

Illustration 8 - Microliths produced by Mesolithic hunters were probably mounted on shafts to make arrows. The left hand drawing is Dr. Pat Stonehouse's sketch of how scalene triangles were probably inserted into arrowshafts as barbs. The microliths from Urra Moor, (Yorkshire) were found as lying above (1). To the right is a reconstruction of what the arrow must have looked like (2). The microliths may have been fixed to the shaft with resin from pine trees. (Reproduced from 'Prehistoric Britain (Archaeology for Schools)' by kind permission of Emeritus Professor Keith Brannigan, Department of Prehistory and Archaeology, University of Sheffield.)

Categories of flint artifacts

Excavated sites reveal many hundreds of flints of varying sizes and shapes. These include 'nodules' of raw flint and chert carried to the site from distant sources and sharp edged 'flakes' and 'blades'. Blades have parallel sides, progressively struck from the nodule, until it has been reduced to a 'core', often cone-shaped. During this process large numbers of very small chips were produced. The object of all this was to make tools, some so small that they must have been mounted in wood, bone or antler, hence 'Microliths'. Flakes and blades could be used as cutting tools, often with blunting on one edge to facilitate handling or mounting, but they were also shaped by secondary flaking into scrapers used for skin and woodwork; burins, used for making incisions into antler, bone and wood; awls for piercing; saws; and microliths which are the points and barbs of arrowshafts, as discussed above.

Axes are found in considerable numbers on many lowland sites but are rare on our moors. These are made from particularly large and high quality flint nodules, the sharp cutting edge being produced by a transverse blow. They can be resharpened by a further transverse blow and the discarded resharpening flakes (axe sharpening flakes or ASFs) are easily recognised. A few such ASFs have been identified in local collections.

One particularily good example came from Ringstone Reservoir, Barkisland, only 8km from Saddleworth, which was found when the water of the Reservoir was low in the summer of 1923 (see Illustration 9). A cast of this axe is held by The Tolson Memorial Museum. (Petch, J. A., *Early Man in The District of Huddersfield)* [37].

Microliths were often made by a special technique that consists of notching one end of a blade and then breaking it obliquely through the notch. This produces two unequal pieces. The smaller piece, called the microburin, was discarded and the larger piece converted by secondary working into a microlith. The object of this was to get rid of the bulge, known as the bulb of percussion, which is present on all intact blades at the end that received the blow which separated it from the core. The term microburin is misleading and is due to the fact that it was originally thought to be a tool in its own right, but this is not so. The presence of microliths helps to identify any flint-assemblage as probably belonging to the Middle Stone Age.

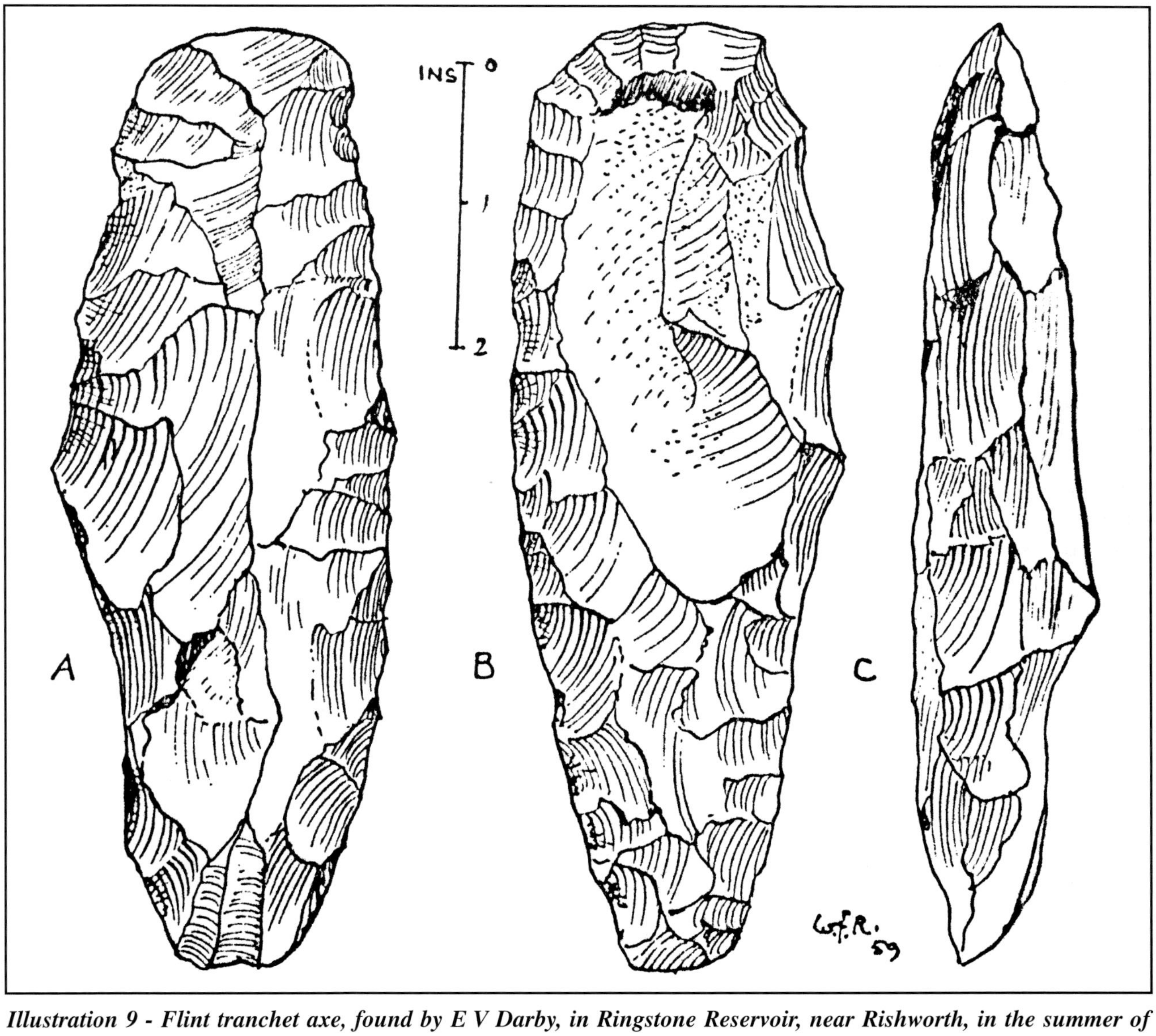

Illustration 9 - Flint tranchet axe, found by E V Darby, in Ringstone Reservoir, near Rishworth, in the summer of 1923 when the water was low. (The word "tranchet" refers to the transversly sharpened cutting edge of the axe.) (Reproduced from the Yorkshire Archaeological Journal, Vol. 40, p. 210, by kind permission of the Hon. Joint Editors of the Y.A.S.)

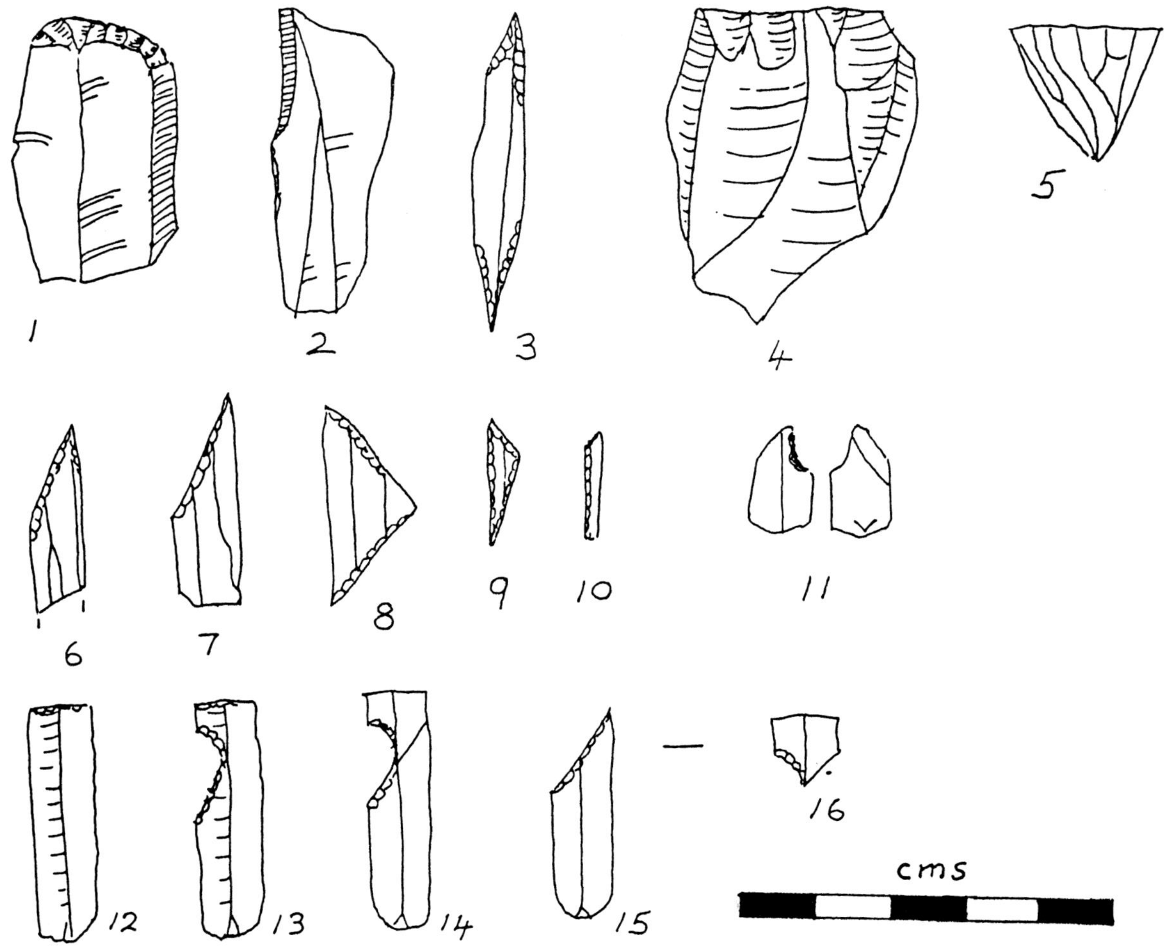

Figure 2

1 - Scraper

2 - Burin

3 - Awl

4,5 - Cores

6,7 - Broad Blade microliths (Obliquely Blunted Points)

8 - Broad Blade microlith (Isosceles triangle)

9 - Narrow Blade microlith - scalene triangle

10 - Narrow Blade microlith - rod

11 - Microburin

12,13,14,15,16 - Microburin technique

12 - blade
13 - notched
14 - broken
15 - Microlith
16 - Microburin (discarded)

Illustration 10 - Mesolithic flint artefacts, including tools, cores and microliths, with a sequence illustrating the "microburin" technique. (Drawing: Dr. Pat Stonehouse. See Sadd. Hist. Soc. Bull., Vol. 15, No.2 , p.21).

Some Mesolithic tools, including a scraper (1), a burin (2), an awl (3), and some microliths (6, 7, 8, 9), together with some cores (4, 5) are shown in Illustration 10, together with a sequence illustrating the 'microburin' technique (12, 13, 14, 15, 16). The easily identifiable characteristics of a microburin are also illustrated, (No. 11) (from SHS Bulletin, Vol.15. no.2. 1985. p.21).

Unfortunately bone or antler does not normally survive in acid upland soils and none has been found in any of our Middle Stone Age sites. However, some lowland sites have much less acid peat and silt conditions, and the site of Star Carr, near Pickering, has helped to fill this gap in our knowledge (Clark, J.G.D., 1954) [39]. Here small groups of Early Middle Stone Age hunters settled on the edge of a lake about 7600 b.c. The bones of their prey have survived and included red deer, roe deer, elk, wild cattle and wild pig. Many of the antler and bone tools they made were also found, including 191 uniserial barbed points, made of red deer antler, six perforated elk antler mattocks, bone pins and so on. Twenty four stag frontlets were also found, with perforations in skull bones, so that they could be fastened to the head. These could possibly have been used in ritual dances or for hunting purposes. Antler and other organic materials had been preserved from decay by waterlogged conditions.

Woodwork included a paddle and the handle of a mattock. Some 30 small shale beads were also found, the shale being pierced by a drill, which appears to have been rotated with great rapidity and precision, probably by using a bow drill.

Similar beads have been found on other Early Mesolithic sites such as Nab Head in Pembrokeshire and Thatcham in Berkshire.

The richness of the finds from Star Carr show how much has been lost from our local sites, where the acid soil conditions only preserve the flint and stone materials, and wood in the form of charcoal.

The Early Middle Stone Age 7600 - 6000 b.c.

This covers the time from the end of the last Ice Age in 8300 b.c. to about 6000 b.c. but there appear to be no northern sites until 7600 b.c. This is a time when, as described above, the climate was of a 'continental' type with rather long cold winters and short sunny summers. Birch was the dominant tree, but towards the end of the period oak, elm and lime were increasing in proportions in the woodlands.

The industry, first described by Francis Buckley and entitled the Broad Blade Industry, was characterised by microliths which were comparatively larger and simpler forms than those of the later Narrow Blade Industry. The most abundant type was that known as the obliquely blunted point, often with some opposed retouch towards the tip (see Illustration 10, drawing No. 6, with retouch, and No. 7 without retouch) but other forms are found including points blunted down the whole of one edge; isosceles triangles (Illustration 10, No.8); and large scalene triangles. These appear to have been the points and barbs of arrow shafts. The rest of the equipment, the scrapers (used for woodwork or scraping hides), burins (used to engrave bone, antler and probably wood), awls, knives, are not sufficiently distinctive to help very much in the identification of different industries. However, the microburin technique appears to have been used a great deal during the Early Mesolithic, and a high percentage of microburins amongst the waste material is a characteristic of Early sites. Flint axes, whose cutting edge is produced by a transverse blow, are quite common in lowland sites, such as Star Carr, but are very rare on upland sites. However, these axes can be resharpened by a further transverse blow, which results in the production of a piece of waste known as an 'axe sharpening flake' (A.S.F), which is easily identified, and such flakes have been found on a number of our early upland sites as mentioned above. The scarcity of axes may be accounted for by reuse, as once broken, the flint would be reworked into smaller tools.

The material of these Early industries in this area is nearly always (90%) a grey or white opaque flint with cherty inclusions, which originates in the chalk of the Yorkshire and Lincolnshire Wolds, some seventy miles distant, but may easily have been collected from glacial erratics deposited in the Vale of Trent. Sites using this material are often described as being of Deepcar type, Deepcar being a semi-lowland site situated on a spur overlooking the junction of the River Porter and the River Don near Sheffield and excavated in 1962 by J. Radley and P. A. Mellars, [40].

There is a less common variant of this Early industry in which the obliquely blunted points are rather broader and never have opposed retouch (Illustration 10, No.7), and points blunted down all of one side are absent. There are other minor differences but the most remarkable difference is that the material may be a translucent brown flint, with a proportion of yellow or grey flint, also translucent, of uncertain source, possibly east coast.

The industry at Star Carr is of this type, as is that of Warcock Hill South excavated by Francis Buckley in the 1920s [38], which lies on the Marsden side of the Pennine Watershed. Another site, 20 yards north of Warcock Hill South, called Turnpike, excavated by the author, proved to have an identical industry (Stonehouse, 1992) [67]. Such paired sites are not uncommon in the early Mesolithic, for example, Pointed Stone 2 and Pointed Stone 3 in the North York Moors (Jacobi 1978) [68], and on the moor just outside Saddleworth to the north of White Hill.

The British Isles were not separated from the continental mainland of Europe until about 6000 b.c. so it is not surprising that there are many sites in Denmark whose industry is similar to that of Deepcar, and others in Holland and North Germany that resemble Star Carr. Presumably there are many sites of both types to be found under the waters of the North Sea.

Early sites are less numerous than Later sites in this area, roughly in the ratio of 1 to 4, and their flint scatter often occupies a greater area than those of Later sites, suggesting that these Early Mesolithic hunters came to our hills in greater numbers, or remained on site for a longer time than the Later Mesolithic peoples.

Comparison of assemblages from upland and lowland sites reveals an interesting difference. Upland sites are generally smaller in area and are dominated by microliths - in other words, by tools which are part of hunting equipment. Lowland sites, such as Turnpike, Warcock Hill North and South, Pule Hill Base, on the other hand, are usually much larger and have a much greater proportion of what may be called domestic tools such as scrapers and burins. A possible explanation of this is that the upland sites were visited on a seasonal basis by small groups or a family party for the purpose of hunting red deer and other prey probably during the summer or late summer months. The larger lowland sites were more in the nature of base camps, possibly occupied throughout the year or during the winter months by a number of different families.

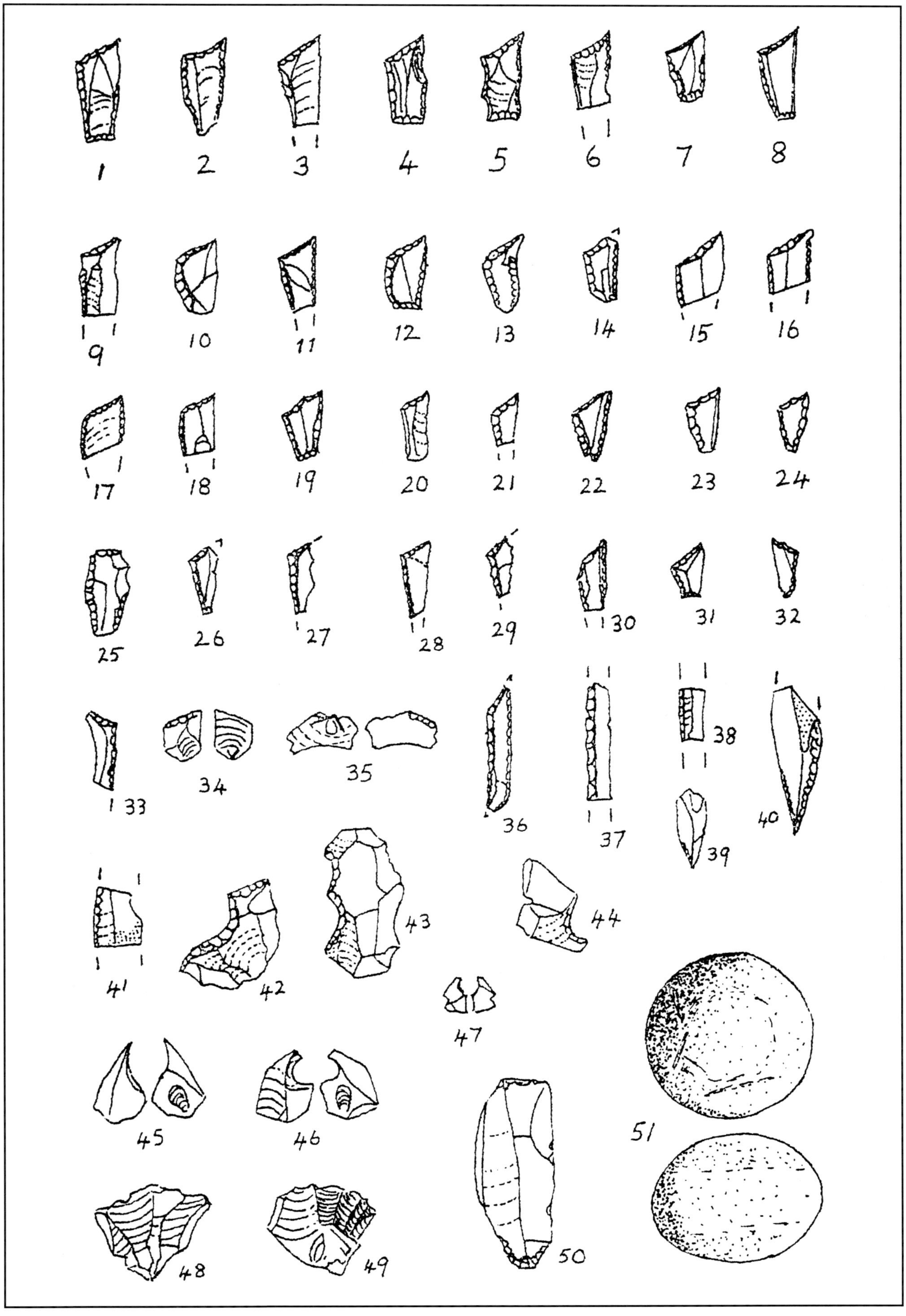

Illustration 11 - Red Ratcher: Material excavated from a late Mesolithic site dominated by trapezoidal shaped microliths. (Drawing: Dr. Pat Stonehouse. See Sadd. Hist. Soc. Bull. Vol. 6, No.2, Reference [94]).

The Later Middle Stone Age 6000 - 3500 b.c.

During this period the climate became warmer and wetter, warmer than it is now. About 6000 b.c. Britain became an island again as rising sea levels flooded the whole of the North Sea Basin, and indeed in some parts of Britain a marine transgression again occurred towards the end of the Middle Stone Age, so that much of the northern Lancashire plain was under water and some river estuaries came further inland.

Birch and pine were now dominated by oak, elm and lime, and alder became much more common although birch persisted on the higher ground. The flint industry changed and the comparatively large Broad Blade microliths were replaced by smaller, delicately made tools - Francis Buckley's 'Narrow Blade' industry - of different, often geometric shapes. They include small scalene triangles (Illustration 10, No.9); backed bladelets ('rods', Illustration 10, No.10); trapezoids where all four sides are of unequal length, and pear shaped points, remarkably small microliths which are indeed pear-shaped and are locally particularly common in the Dean Clough area.

Later sites are often dominated by one or other of these point types to the virtual exclusion of the others so that it is reasonable to talk of a 'triangle' site or a 'rod' site. Very small triangles are particularly common on March Hill and are sometimes referred to as 'March Hill Triangles'.

A site dominated by trapezoidal microliths was Red Ratcher, Grid Reference SE 058036 on the northern edge of Little Clough, a triburary stream of Crowden Great Brook. The site was excavated by the author with Saddleworth Historical Society in the early 1970s. Illustration 11 shows clearly the trapezoidal shapes of the flint material [94].

The material used is often a beautiful, translucent honey coloured flint, but brown, grey, yellow and pink flints also occur, whose source may be the glacial drift of the east coast. The mixture of colours of these late assemblages is sometimes quite startling. High quality black chert of Derbyshire origin also occurs and some assemblages consist entirely of this material. This contrasts sharply with Early assemblages where black chert does occur but in much smaller quantities.

Some Later sites contain rhyolite. This raw material was first recognised on a Mesolithic site by Stephen Poole at his site at Piethorne Brook, where it formed the majority of the artefacts (605 out of a total of 1077) (Greater Manchester Archaeological Journal, 1986) [5].

Rhyolite, a volcanic rock, originates in the Borrowdale Volcanic Series of the Lake District and is a fairly common component of the glacial drift of Lancashire and Cheshire, and has been found locally. (Barnes, B., 1982) [59].

The great interest of this observation is that it suggests a link with the west, so that it is possible that small groups from both east and west of the Pennine watershed visited our hills.

Such groups might have belonged to different territories. The narrow watershed between the east and west in our area might well have been a suitable place for a meeting between these different groups for social purposes (rituals, marriage, barter, etc.). D. Spratt has suggested that this might have occurred at the west-east watershed on the North York Moors [33]. Such meetings of different tribes may help to explain the high density of sites in our area.

The picture that emerges for both the Early and Late Mesolithic is that of small groups of hunter-gatherers armed with bows and arrows and probably accompanied by dogs, spending the

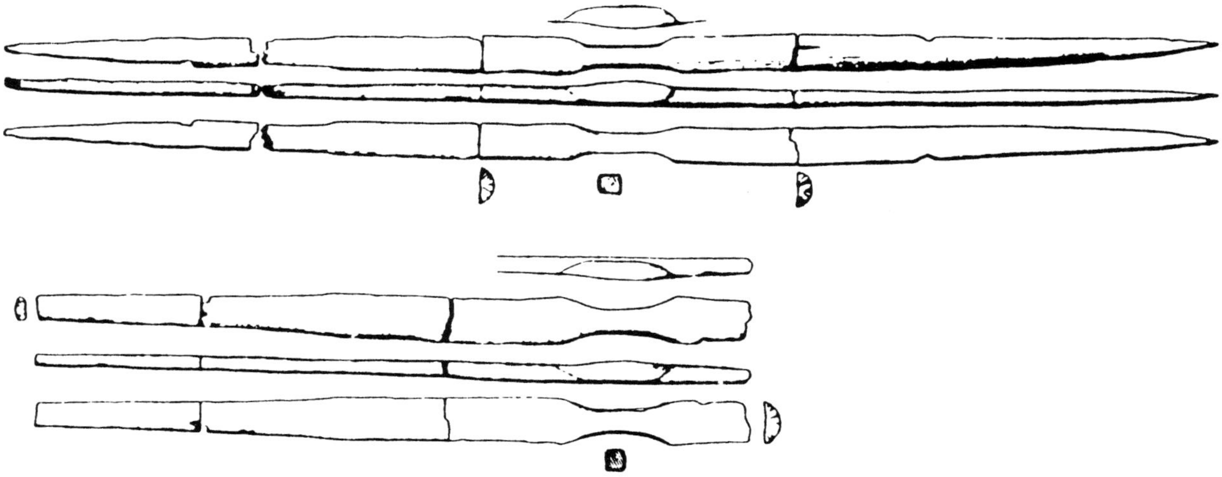

Mesolithic bows from Holmegaard, Denmark (approx. $\frac{1}{8}$ full size)

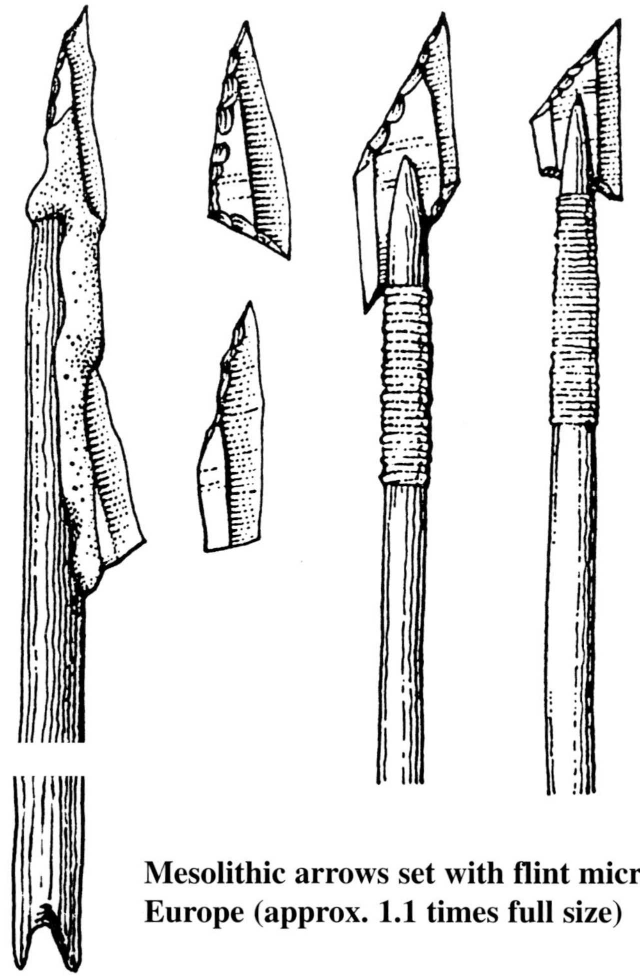

Mesolithic arrows set with flint microliths, from north-west Europe (approx. 1.1 times full size)

Illustration 12 - Evidence of Mesolithic archery. (Reproduced from publications of the late Sir Grahame Clark, by kind permission of his literary executor, Professor P. A. Mellars, Professor of Archaeology and President of Corpus Christi College, Cambridge University).

winter in larger settlements in the lowlands, but undertaking expeditions to the uplands in the late summer to hunt red deer, roe deer and wild cattle. They would no doubt exploit the edible wild plants in the form of bulbs, roots, rhizomes, tubers, berries and nuts. It is difficult to obtain direct evidence for this, but certainly hazel nuts, often charred, are commonly found on Mesolithic sites, including one Later site slightly to the north of White Hill which produced 200 fragments (Stephen Poole - personal communication).

Mesolithic man used the bow and arrow, but no bows or arrowshafts have been found on our hills. A bow found in a Danish site (Holmegaard IV) of Mesolithic age and made from elm, was about 1.5m long and shaped in the middle to provide a hand grip and notched at either end for a bow string.

Arrow shafts have also been found abroad; one, also of Mesolithic age, came from Loshult in Sweden. It had a tip and barb made of flint, resin being used to fix the flint to the shaft (Fig 3, p 47, *Mesolithic Prelude*, Clark, J.G.D.) [82]. These bows and arrowshafts may be seen on Illustration 12.

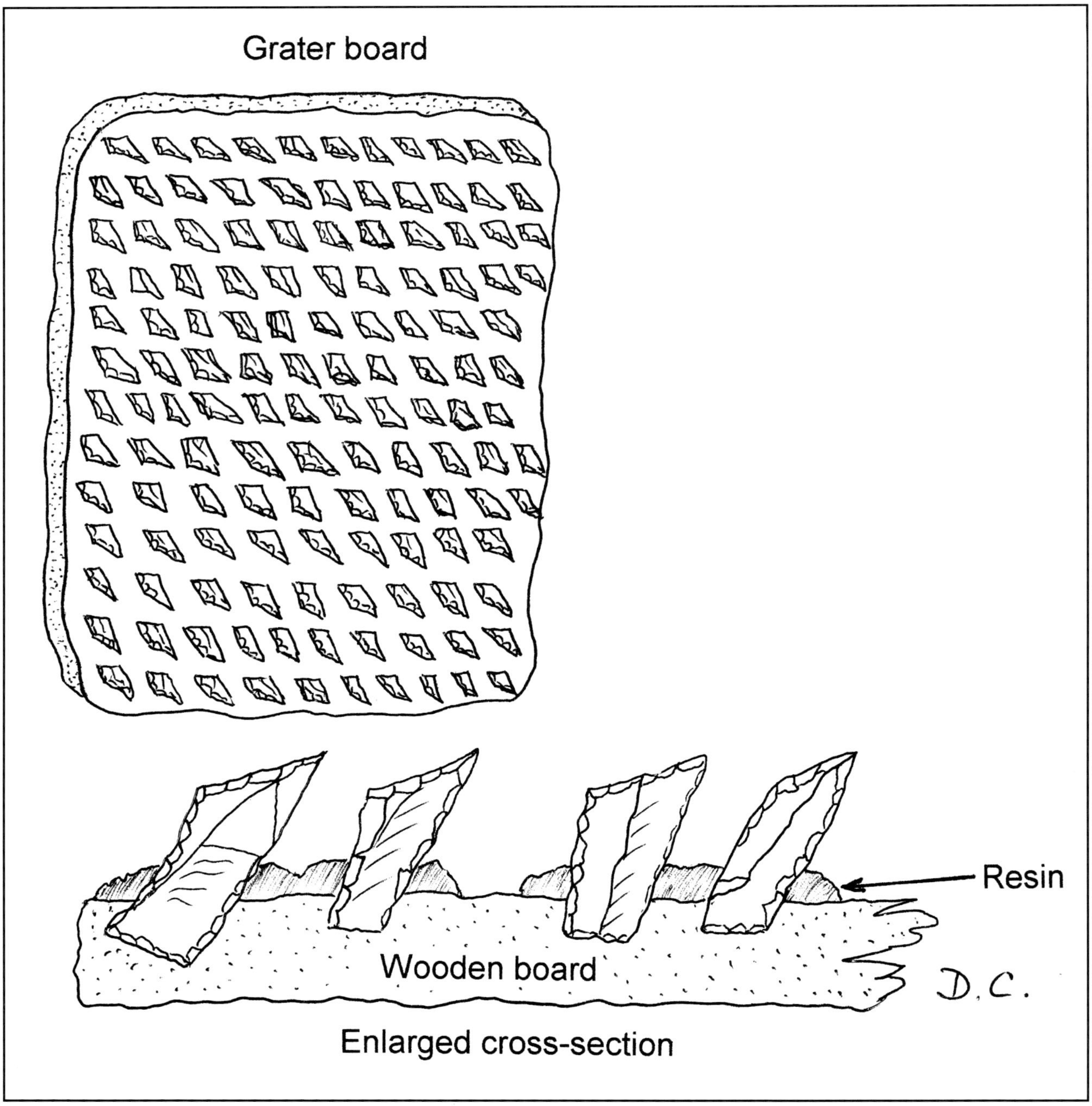

Illustration 13 - Suggested use of Late Mesolithic trapezoidal points set into a board to make a grater. (After Clarke, D. L., 'Mesolithic Europe - The Economic Basis', reference [60]).

It is assumed that the small scalene triangles of the Later Mesolithic were inserted into the shafts of arrows to provide barbs as shown in Illustration 8 (see page 26), and such triangles have indeed been found in straight rows, but have never been actually found attached to an arrowshaft.

Another view was put forward by David Clarke ('Mesolithic Europe - The Economic Basis', 1976) [60] who has argued that many of the microliths were fixed in large numbers into a board to form an instrument for plant processing. There is ethnographic evidence for the existence of such composite grater boards from the forests of S. America, Africa and S. E. Asia. (See Illustration 13).

However, it seems reasonably clear that much of Mesolithic man's activity was indeed concerned with the hunting of woodland game, and cave drawings from Eastern Spain frequently depict the hunting of red deer and wild cattle using bows and barbed arrow shafts. The dating of these paintings is uncertain, although they certainly seem to depict a Mesolithic life style.

It seems probable therefore that the microliths were used as barbs and points on arrowshafts at least in this area, and, as mentioned above, they have been found mounted in this fashion in Sweden.

Chronology

Accurate dating of these sites is very difficult and is based mainly on the radiocarbon assay of charcoal. The upland mineral soil is only a few inches thick so stratigraphy has little to offer in separating flint assemblages into periods.

Pollen analysis in other parts of Britain and on the continent suggests that Broad Blade sites were occupied at a time when the environment was dominated by birch and pine, whilst Narrow Blade sites are associated with oak and elm and (in some areas) lime, although as mentioned above, birch persisted at the higher levels.

Radiocarbon dating has been carried out at a number of local sites, including six excavated by Francis Buckley where the charcoal had been collected in the 1920s. The results are given in Table 2 and are certainly in agreement with those from other parts of the country and suggest that Broad Blade sites are indeed older than Narrow Blade ones, but there is always the possibility of contamination from earlier and later horizons. Moreover, the validity of results from charcoal obtained in the 1920s and stored under uncertain conditions has been questioned. (Francis Buckley's charcoal was sealed in glass topped boxes in the 1920s.)

There is some evidence that 'rods' became common in the later part of the Late Mesolithic Age. Rocher Moss South 2 (Stonehouse, 1980) [41] and Dunford Bridge B., (a site on the Sheffield moors) [42] were dated to 3880 ±100 b.c and 3430 ± 80 b.c. respectively.

Table 2: RADIOCARBON DATES FOR LOCAL SITES			
Site	**Industry**	**Lab. Number**	**Date**
* Lominot III	Broad Blade	Q1187	7615 ± 470 b.c.
Waystone Edge	Broad Blade	Q1300	7446 ± 210 b.c.
* Warcock Hill South	Broad Blade	Q1185	7260 ± 340 b.c.
* Warcock Hill Site 3	Triangle Site	Q789	6660 ± 110 b.c.
Dean Clough Site 1	Triangle Site	Q1299	5645 ± 140 b.c.
Rishworth Drain 2	Triangle Site	Q1166	5600 ± 210 b.c.
* March Hill 2	Triangle Site	Q1188	4070 ± 220 b.c.
* March Hill 2	Triangle Site	Q788	3900 ± 80 b.c.
* Lominot IV	Triangle Site	Q1189	3660 ± 120 b.c.
Rocher Moss South 2	Rod Site	Q1190	3880 ± 120 b.c.
# Dan Clough	Triangle Site	Groningen 12278	5750 ± 70 b.p.

Editor's note: Dr. Pat Stonehouse asked that the dates in this table be left unchanged so that there was a record of his original paper. Tables of corrected dates, adjusted to reflect recent advances in radiocarbon dating accuracy, with explanations, appear in Appendix 2.

Author's Notes
**These are Buckley sites excavated in the 1920s, the radiocarbon assay being carried out on charcoal, stored in the Tolson Memorial Museum, Huddersfield.*

 # Dan Clough - Note that the figure given is not b.c. but b.p.; that is 'before present' (ie 1950.) This may well be the most accurate figure in this list, as the tests were made on charcoal which came from a hearth, clearly defined by upright burned slabs, floored by stone slabs and sealed by peat. (Stephen Poole, personal communication).

Summary

It is difficult to paint a picture of what these people were like physically, as practically no skeletal remains have been found in Britain apart from one found in Gough's Cave in the Cheddar Gorge. This was at first thought to belong to the Ice Age, but gave a carbon 14 date of 9080 ±150 b.p.- in other words, about 7000 b.c. and puts it firmly in the Earlier Mesolithic.

Some fifty skeletons were found in 1804 in Aveline's Hole, another cave in the Mendip Hills. Most of these were destroyed during an air raid on Bristol in 1941, but appear to be Mesolithic, according to two radiocarbon assays carried out on surviving long bones.

The fairly recent discovery [43] of a Late Middle Stone Age Cemetery in Zeeland, Denmark, produced 23 individuals dated to about 4000 B.C. The males were reasonably robust, with an average height of 5' 7" (170 cm) which is nearly 3" (7cm) taller than the mean height of the farmers of the following Danish New Stone Age. This is in accord with evidence from other sources and suggests that hunting/gathering peoples fed better and had better general health than their farming successors.

Excavations at Skateholm, Sweden in 1980-84 revealed a combination of a settlement area and a cemetery (Larsson, 1985/1990) [71].

Clothing was probably animal skin. Hunting methods included the use of dogs and the use of bows and arrows. Some of the bows have survived in Scandinavia and are beautifully and skilfully made.

In Scandinavia there is evidence for deep sea fishing, probably from dug out canoes or skin boats, and complicated fishing traps have also survived at some sites.

In general these people were obviously both intelligent and enterprising, adjusting themselves with great success to the changing environment, and it was people at this level of technology who in different parts of the world began about 10,000 years ago to adopt cultivation of plants and domesticate some animals.

Recent studies show that people who live by hunting and foraging have a better diet and more leisure time than those who practice primitive subsistence farming. It was probably not lack of knowledge or intelligence that prevented hunter/foragers from developing farming, but rather lack of motivation. The great advantage of farming is that it can support a much greater population and it may have been population increase that forced the change; probably tentatively at first, with many false starts.

It is possible that our local Mesolithic population, few though they were, may have been feeling their way towards the manipulation of some animals, such as red deer.

The evidence, such as it is, is that small quantities of charcoal are to be found in the soil beneath the peat all over our moors, and in larger quantities in the vicinity of Mesolithic sites.

Moreover, there is evidence of clearance in the neighbourhood of sites, as judged by pollen evidence from the Mesolithic levels in the soil.

This might suggest the regular burning of areas of woodland, in particular at high altitudes, which would help to explain the failure of the woodland canopy in this area to reach the heights that it does in the North Pennines and the Lake District, where levels of 2500 feet (760 metres) have been found, (Simmons, I. G.) [86], p.20, compared to about 1400 feet (430 metres) in the South Pennines.

The advantages would be that this would impose a certain degree of predictability on the movements of herds of deer and also provide more readily available browse, and lead to artificial concentrations of deer which could be exploited and perhaps to some extent controlled. (Mellars, P. A., 1976) [69].

Thus Mesolithic man may well have permanently altered the Pennine environment by creating semi-permanent openings in the tree cover, which would allow the soil to undergo 'leaching', which in turn would result in impoverished acid soils on which blanket bog might spread. (Acid soils and blanket bog form as a result of blocked drainage arising from the formation of an impervious iron pan lower down in the soil horizon).

It seems therefore that our wild, treeless, peat covered moorlands may owe their character in some degree to the activities of these small groups of hunter/gatherers who visited our hills thousands of years ago as the climate became wetter and 'Atlantic' in character.

CHAPTER TWO

Neolithic (The New Stone Age)

Early 3500 - 2500 b.c.
Later 2500 - 1700 b.c.

Middle Stone Age man was a hunter/gatherer who let nature do all the hard work but at the cost of having few possessions, usually with no permanent home and having to adjust his activities to the seasons.

The superiority of the farming way of life seems self-evident so it comes as a surprise that recent research shows that even modern hunter/gatherers often live better and have more leisure than primitive subsistence farmers (Sahlins, M., *Stone Age Economics*) [46]. It seems probable it was not lack of knowledge but rather lack of motivation that led mankind to keep to the old hunting ways for so long. As mentioned earlier, the spur, the motivation, was probably an increase in numbers - in other words, overpopulation.

Farming appears to have started in a number of different centres, isolated from each other, including some in the New World; and at varying dates after the end of the last Ice Age, (8000 b.c.).

In the Middle East farming began about 8000 b.c. It may have spread by a process of diffusion and perhaps colonisation into Eastern Europe and along the fertile and easily tilled loess lands of the Danube and the Rhine, to reach the Atlantic seaboard and the North Sea by about 4000 B.C. and then to Britain.

However, wild cattle and wild pigs were present in Western Europe, including Britain, and red deer, a social animal, may have been subjected to some degree of control by the local populations, so that there is always a possibility that the process may have been much more complicated than that of simple colonisation with boat loads of immigrants arriving on our shores with their domesticated animals and cereals from the continent. Wheat and barley, however, must have been introduced as they are not indigenous to Europe and this is also probably true of sheep and goats.

There is evidence that farming was being practised in Britain by 3500 b.c. New artifact technology appears, such as ground stone axes and pottery. Sickles and querns show that cereal crops were being grown in suitable areas that had fertile soils, their presence being confirmed by pollen analysis. Pollen analysis also shows that openings were being made in the forest, initially perhaps mainly by fire, but also by axe, and by 3000 b.c. large areas of open land had been created, especially on light and fertile soils such as in chalklands and in limestone areas such as the Lincolnshire and Yorkshire Wolds - and the Peak District and Craven.

The bones of domesticated animals (cattle, pigs and sheep) are to be found on the earliest sites.

These farmers soon began to undertake communal engineering projects such as ‘causewayed enclosures’, which consist of a series of concentric ditches with internal banks which are broken by numerous causeways with pottery, animal bones and domestic refuse stratified in the ditches. These are found mainly in the south of England and are often situated on gentle hill tops, but lowland sites are not uncommon.

'Long barrows' were constructed, made of earth and often containing a mortuary house made of wood, and enclosing burials. These are to be found over much of Britain, including Yorkshire, but in those parts of the country where stone outcrops occur, somewhat similar structures made of stone appear, but always containing chambers where the dead could be housed. Round mounds also appear in some parts of the British Isles enclosing a burial chamber approached by a passage. Some of these structures are enormous - the amount of material contained in the Newgrange burial chamber in Ireland is 200,000 tons.

A change occurred about 2500 b.c. From this time onwards causewayed enclosures, long barrows and megalithic burial chambers ceased to be built, but other structures began to appear, such as cursuses, which consist of a long avenue defined by two parallel earthen banks with ditches outside them and closed at the ends. The Dorset cursus is six miles long and must have required an enormous amount of labour - as did Silbury Hill in Wiltshire which is 130 feet high, covers $5\frac{1}{4}$ acres and is the largest prehistoric structure in Europe.

Another ritual monument, the 'henge', which in its most typical form consists of a circular area surrounded by a ditch with an outside bank and two opposed entrances, is to be found from Orkney to Cornwall. Related structures, which are not circular, such as Durrington Walls, can be of enormous size.

The nearest henges to Saddleworth are in the limestone Peak District at the Bull Ring at Doveholes, 3 miles to the NE of Buxton, and Arbor Low, 5 miles to the SW of Bakewell, both in Derbyshire. Stone circles (some within henges), stone alignments and large standing stones were also erected during this period and persisted into the Bronze Age.

Pottery, which in the Early Neolithic was thin walled and lacked ornamentation, developed richly decorated forms in the Later Neolithic, as exemplified by Peterborough Ware and Grooved Ware. Beakers appear for the first time at the end of the New Stone Age, but are discussed more fully in Chapter 3, the Bronze Age.

The ground stone axes, mentioned above, were made from flint or hard igneous or metamorphic rocks. The sources of most of these rocks are known, the two richest sources being Great Langdale, in the Lake District, and Graig Lwyd, near Penmaenmawr in North Wales.

The axes were roughed out by flaking or pecking, and then finished by a process of grinding, and then hafted to make a very serviceable tool, suitable for tree cutting. Flint axes were polished in the same manner, the flint itself being later mined by shafts so as to reach flint layers undamaged by frost.

Copper was being utilised by 2150 b.c. at a time when the early Beakers were making their appearance, and communal burial was being replaced by individual burial in round mounds.

These Beakers were well made vessels, flat bottomed, and ornamented over much of their surface.

This is a time when the marginal nature of the Central Pennines becomes very obvious. Farming, especially arable farming, was difficult, so this area was poor and relatively unexploited when compared with the limestone district of Derbyshire to the south with its two henges, megalithic burial chambers and settlements, or the chalk area of the Yorkshire Wolds to the east with its great burial mounds like Duggleby Howe and Willy Howe: its long barrows and cursuses and the tallest standing stone in Britain at Rudston.

Illustration 14 - Later Neolithic transverse arrowheads. Left, found on Pule Hill by F. Buckley in 1935, Right, found on Rocher Moss by Dr. G. B. Buckley in 1935. (Photograph taken by Barbara Booth of part of the Saddleworth Museum Collection with the kind permission of the Curator, Matthew Richardson). (Approx. 3.5 times full size).

No earthworks or settlements of this period have been found in Saddleworth and only a few in the surrounding area. These include the Later Neolithic hill top occupation sites at Castle Hill, Almondbury near Huddersfield, (Varley, W. J., 1976) [27] and at Castle Hill, Denby near Huddersfield, (Gilks, J.A., 1974) [55], both on the drier eastern side of the Pennine watershed.

However, there is evidence for Neolithic activity in Saddleworth. Arrowheads are not infrequently found on the moors, usually in isolation. These are of two main types: leaf-shaped and related lozenge shaped arrowheads beautifully made with shallow retouch on both sides, and transverse arrowheads, which do not pierce but have a cutting edge.

Transverse arrowheads belong to the Later Neolithic and are particularly associated with Grooved Ware (Smith, I. F., 1974) [56] (see illustrations 14 and 15).

Greater importance must be attached to the presence of ground stone and flint axe/adzes, a number of which have been found in Saddleworth and which are described below.

Stone axes, as already mentioned, are made of fine, hard, ashy, igneous or metamorphic rocks which behave much as flint, a compact variety of chalcedony silica, when struck. They are obtained from many different sources (axe factories) and it is often possible to determine the source by petrological study.

Fifty-four axes from the Central Pennines have undergone such petrological examination - of which twenty-two are of Cumbrian origin; four are from Graig Lwyd in North Wales; three from Tievebulliagh in Northern Ireland; two from the Whin Sill of Northern England; and one each from Cornwall, South-West Wales and the Nuneaton district (Barnes, 1982) [1].

Flint axes and adzes have to be made from large nodules of unflawed high quality flint. Surface material and beach pebbles are unsuitable so the material has to be obtained by mining in Southern England - but large enough flint blocks occur in the glacial clays of the east coast for axe making. Shafts up to forty feet deep are sunk until a suitable band of flint is found and then galleries made laterally in order to extract the material.

Such mines are not uncommon in the South and East of England - examples include Cissbury, Blackpatch and Church Hill in Sussex and Grimes Graves in Norfolk. Some date from well before 3000 b.c. (circa 4000 B.C.).

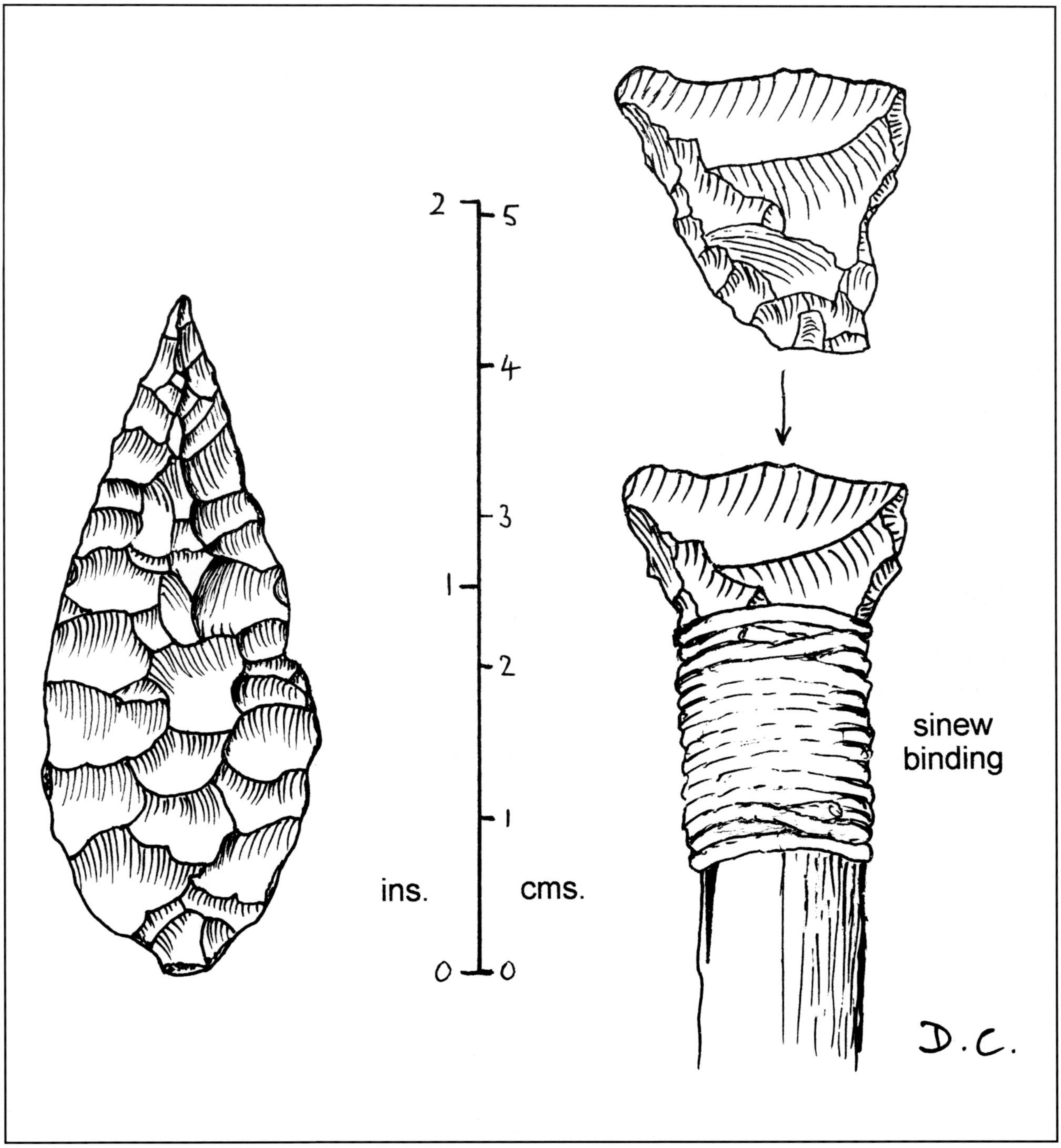

Illustration 15 - Left: a leaf shaped Neolithic arrowhead, taken from the photograph of Francis Buckley's find on Buckstones Moor in Fig. 16, p. 43 of 'Early Man in the District of Huddersfield', by J A Petch, [37], (by kind permission of the Kirklees Community History Service at The Tolson Memorial Museum, Huddersfield.) Right: A transverse arrowhead, showing possible method of binding to a split wooden arrowshaft with sinew. (Drawing: D. Chadderton).

Illustration 16 - Ammon Wrigley's drawings of the Upper Castleshaw Reservoir axe (upper print, 1.2 times actual size) and the Cudworth Quarry axe (lower print, 0.9 times actual size). (Reproduced from 'Saddleworth: Its Prehistoric Remains', by kind permission of Christine Seville and Ruth E Greenwood).

Details of Axes from Saddleworth & Adjacent Areas

Castleshaw Upper Reservoir

SD998100 800 ft (244 metres) O.D.

(Broadhead Reservoir)

This axe is described and illustrated by Ammon Wrigley in his book - *Saddleworth - Its Prehistoric Remains* (1911) [10]. A finely polished axe made of greenstone, it was found six feet below ground level when the reservoir was being constructed in 1899. It is 4.5" (114mm) long and 2.5" (64mm) wide and has its lateral edges flattened. A plaster cast was in Rochdale Museum. (See Illustration 16).

Cudworth Quarry

SE 000110 1220 ft (372 Metres) O.D.

Ammon Wrigley also describes and illustrates this in - *Saddleworth - Its Prehistoric Remains*, Plate I, opposite p.35 and so does Brierley, J., (1910) *Prehistoric Saddleworth*, Plates V and VI [88]. The axe is 7" (178mm) long, 3" (76mm) wide and has its butt end broken. It was found in a cleft in rock at a height of 1220 ft O.D. in 1887. In section the lateral edges are flattened, which is quite common in 'Cumbrian' axes. Sometimes called 'Cumbrian Clubs', they are products of the Langdale Group of axe factories in the Lake District. There is a good cast of this axe in the Rochdale Museum.

According to Ammon Wrigley the axe was seen by Mr. S Sydney Platt, then Borough Surveyor in Rochdale, who considered that it was made out of diorite. Lawrence Keen and V. Radley describe it as being made of greenstone. Report on the Petrological Identification of Stone Axes in Yorkshire, PPMS 1971 XXXVII.

Lark Hill Farm

SD99430749 950 feet (289 metres) O.D.

This polished stone axe was found in 1959 during work on a field wall near Lark Hill Farm. It is 7" (178mm) long and $2\frac{3}{4}$" (70mm) wide at the cutting edge and also has its lateral edges flattened, and is described as being made of greenstone (Keen and Radley, 1971), Greenstone (Group VI) in Barnes, 1982, *Man and The Changing Landscape*, App. 2, Note 123 [1]. Report on the Petrological Identification of Stone Axes from Yorkshire, PPHS 1971, XXXVIII (see Illustration 17).

Dean Clough, near Denshaw

SD 9812 c. 1000 ft (305 metres) O.D.

This is the butt end of a flaked flint axe, $4\frac{5}{8}$" (117mm) long with its cutting edge broken in antiquity. Greyish patina. (Barnes, 1982, *Man and the Changing Landscape*, App. 2, 122). Tolson Memorial Museum, Huddersfield. 23.1.66. T.M.M. Index.

The map reference gives a position in a very steep valley leading into Crooked Gate Reservoir, but if it is an approximate map reference, it might be on the neighbouring moorland flats.

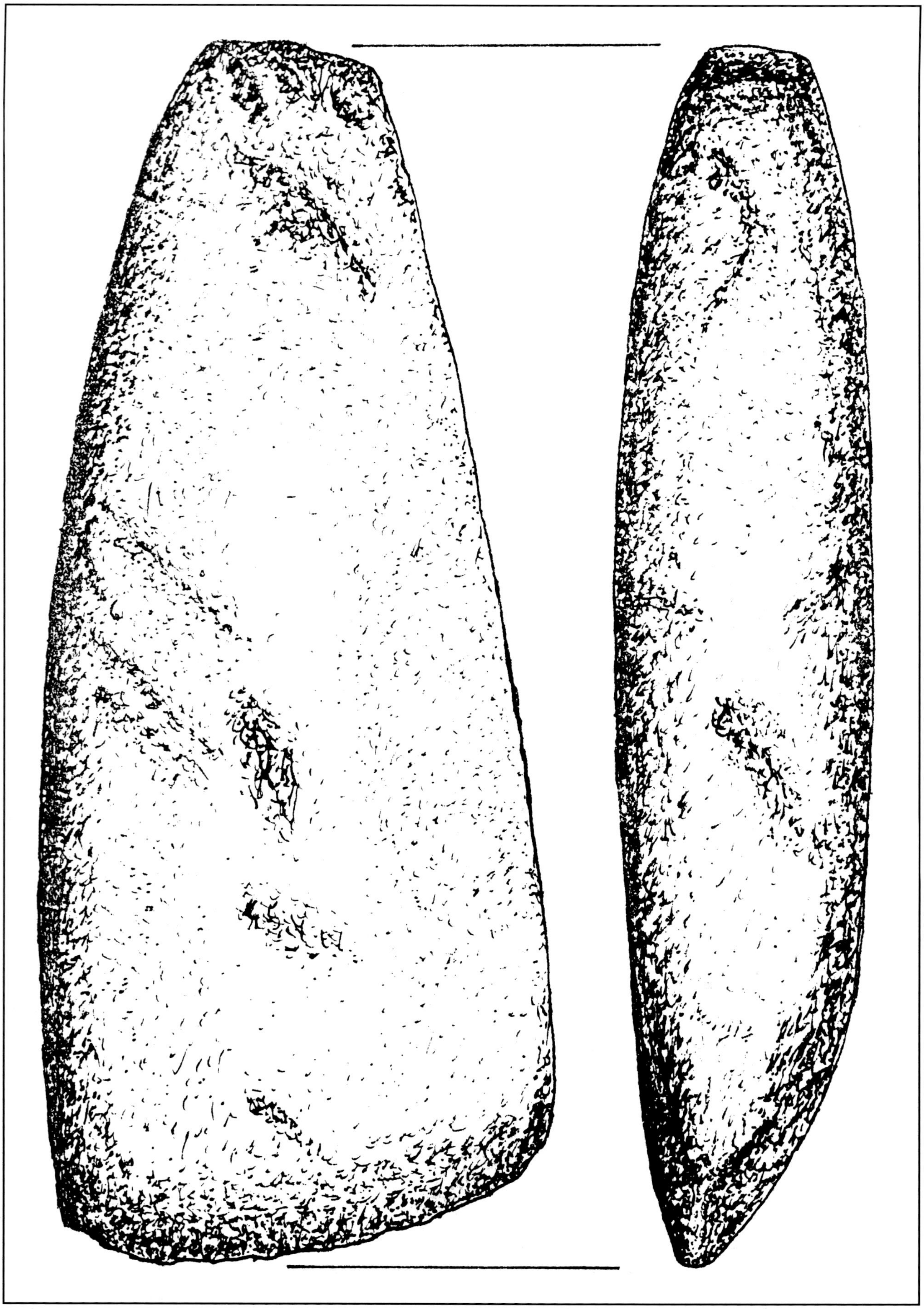

Illustration 17 - The Lark Hill Farm axe (Drawing by Alec Schofield, reproduced by kind permission of Phyllis Schofield). (1.25 times actual size).

Dean Clough, near Denshaw

SD 994127   1400 ft (662 metres) O.D.

This flint axe was found in 1989 by Lee Cherry, projecting from a bank, some 70 metres south of Readycon Dean Brook.

It is $5\frac{1}{4}$" (133mm) long and 2" (51mm) wide at the cutting edge and is made of what at first appears to be cream coloured flint, but is seen to be grey where a flake has been broken off in recent times. Originally a completely ground flint axe with the lateral edges flattened, both the butt end and the cutting edge are battered by re-use as a hammer. In its present condition it could not be used as a cutting tool. In private possession. (Illustrated on Colour Plate 1, on page 53).

Greenfield Brook

SE 0204?   600 ft (183 metres) O.D.

Stone axe. $3\frac{5}{8}$" (92mm) long: $1\frac{3}{8}$" (35mm) wide at the cutting edge, found by Mr Fred Allen of Greenfield in the brook. It has a pecked surface with a polished cutting edge. Greenstone or possibly porcellanite of Irish origin.

Tolson Memorial Museum, Huddersfield (A.19.58) (Barnes, 1982, Appendix 2, Note 123). Given a different and unlikely grid reference in 'Stone Axe Studies' Vol. 2. and described as metadolerite. (Research Report for C.B.A. No. 67, 1988, eds. T. H. McK. Clough and W. A. Cummins, p.210, No. 176.) [96]. (See Illustration 18, upper).

Luzley, Mossley, Tameside

SD 0196

A 'good specimen of a stone celt' was found near Luzley, Mossley, by Seth Radcliffe, postmaster of Upper Mossley (Trans. Lancs. & Ches. Antiq. Soc. 14, 1896, 162). There is a sketch of this axe in 'The Story of Mossley', compiled and illustrated by Alfred Holt (1974). According to his account the axe was found on the hill top in the field known as 'Featherbed', on Light Birches, and was $7\frac{1}{2}$" (191mm) long and $4\frac{1}{2}$" (114mm) wide at the cutting edge.

The Medlock flint adze, and a small flint axe from Green Withens on Rishworth Moor, together with a polished discoidal flint knife from Slatepit Moor, near Carr Clough, Mossley, all appear to belong to the Late Neolithic, and although not found in Saddleworth, are all from find spots near the Saddleworth boundary, and are described in greater detail below. (See Illustration 18, lower).

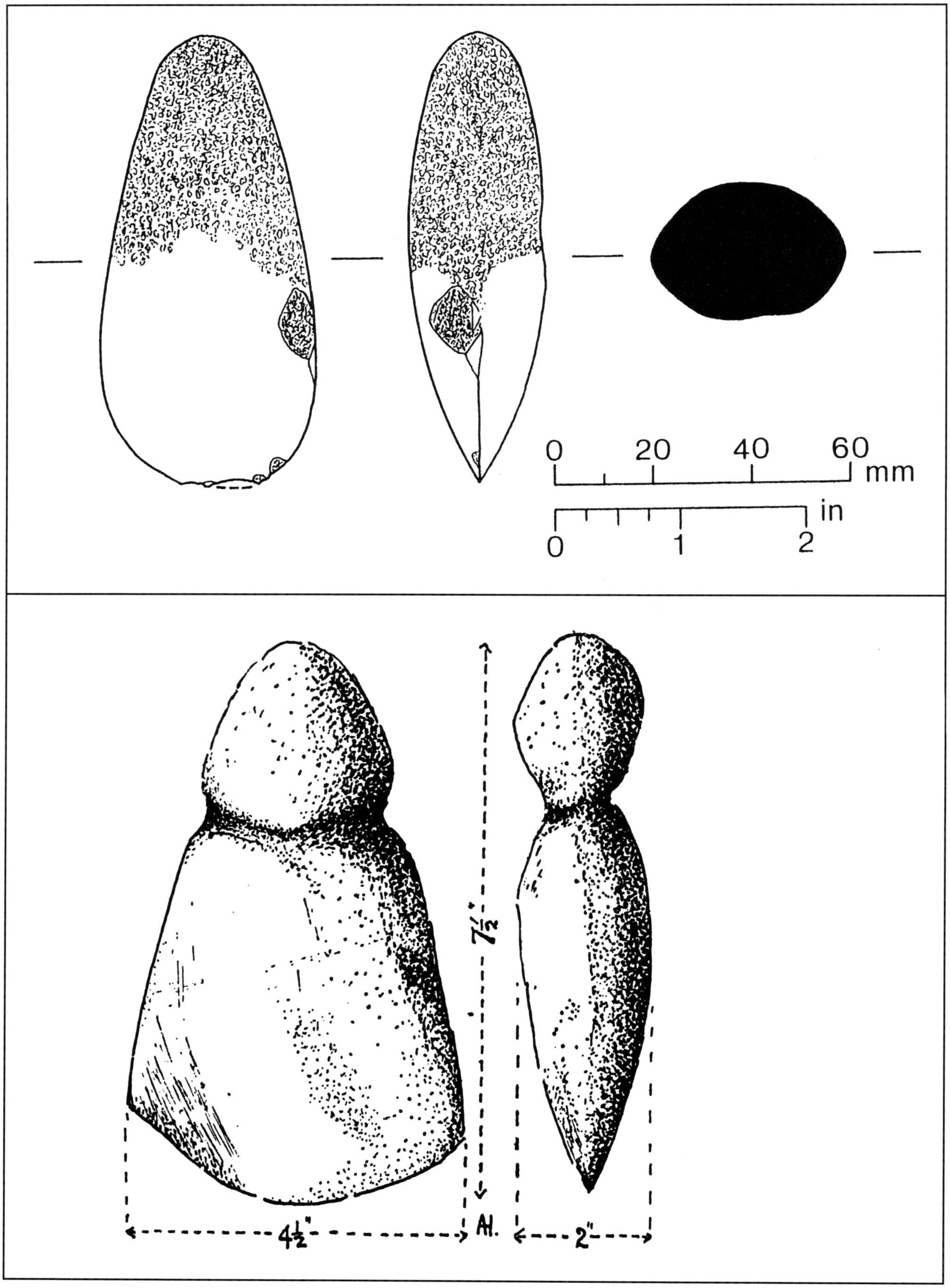

Illustration 18 - (Upper) The Neolithic polished stone axe from Greenfield Brook, found by Fred Allen. (Drawn by J. A. Gilks).

(Lower) The Luzley axe, found by Mossley postmaster, Seth Radcliffe. (Drawing taken from 'The Story of Mossley' by Alfred Holt, and reproduced by kind permission of The Mossley Civic Society).

Medlock Flint Adze, Oldham

SD94850335 475 feet (145 metres) O.D.

This adze was found in 1980 by Michael Crompton, aged 11 years, projecting from the right bank of the River Medlock at a point below Holts Mill some five miles from its source. Somewhat clumsy in appearance (see illustration 19), it is $5\frac{1}{2}$" (140mm) long, 2" (48mm) at its widest and $1\frac{3}{4}$" (44mm) at its not very obvious waist. In private possession. (See reference [54]) The flint is a very attractive golden brown with two darker bands, there is a small residual polished area near the cutting edge.

It seems probable that this polished area formerly extended across the whole breadth of the cutting edge and that its present condition is the result of its use as a working implement.

Another example of a flint adze in the Central Pennines is in the Museum of the Natural History Society of Bacup. This was found on Tooter Hill at an altitude of 1450 feet (442 Metres) O.D. (See reference 54.) This is elegantly waisted and of a type associated with high status Late Neolithic burials and classified as a 'Duggleby Adze' from the type site in East Yorkshire. (See T.G.Manby, 1974, 'Grooved Ware Sites in Yorkshire and the North of England', Brit. Arch. Reps. 9, p 98) [52].

The Medlock adze is of inferior workmanship but also belongs to the Late Neolithic.

Polished stone and flint axes and adzes apart from the above, have, of course, been found in adjoining areas, including four from Rochdale (Wardle, Hollingworth Lake, Castle Hill - near the centre of Rochdale - and New Hey), and one from Royton.

The eastern side of the Pennines has produced greater numbers. Twenty have been found in the Metropolitan District of Kirklees; twelve from Calderdale, five of these from Rishworth Moor, a significant concentration.

The Sheffield City Museum has a stone Axe Hammer found at Thorpe, Almondbury. Accession No. J.1, the original donation was to The Sheffield Philosophical Society. It is the only complete example from the Huddersfield district, as the Kirkburton example has been broken and reperforated, comparable with the Axe Hammer accompanying the Milnrow Cremation burial. (Rochdale Museum)[8]

---

[8] *This paragraph was kindly contributed by T G Manby.*

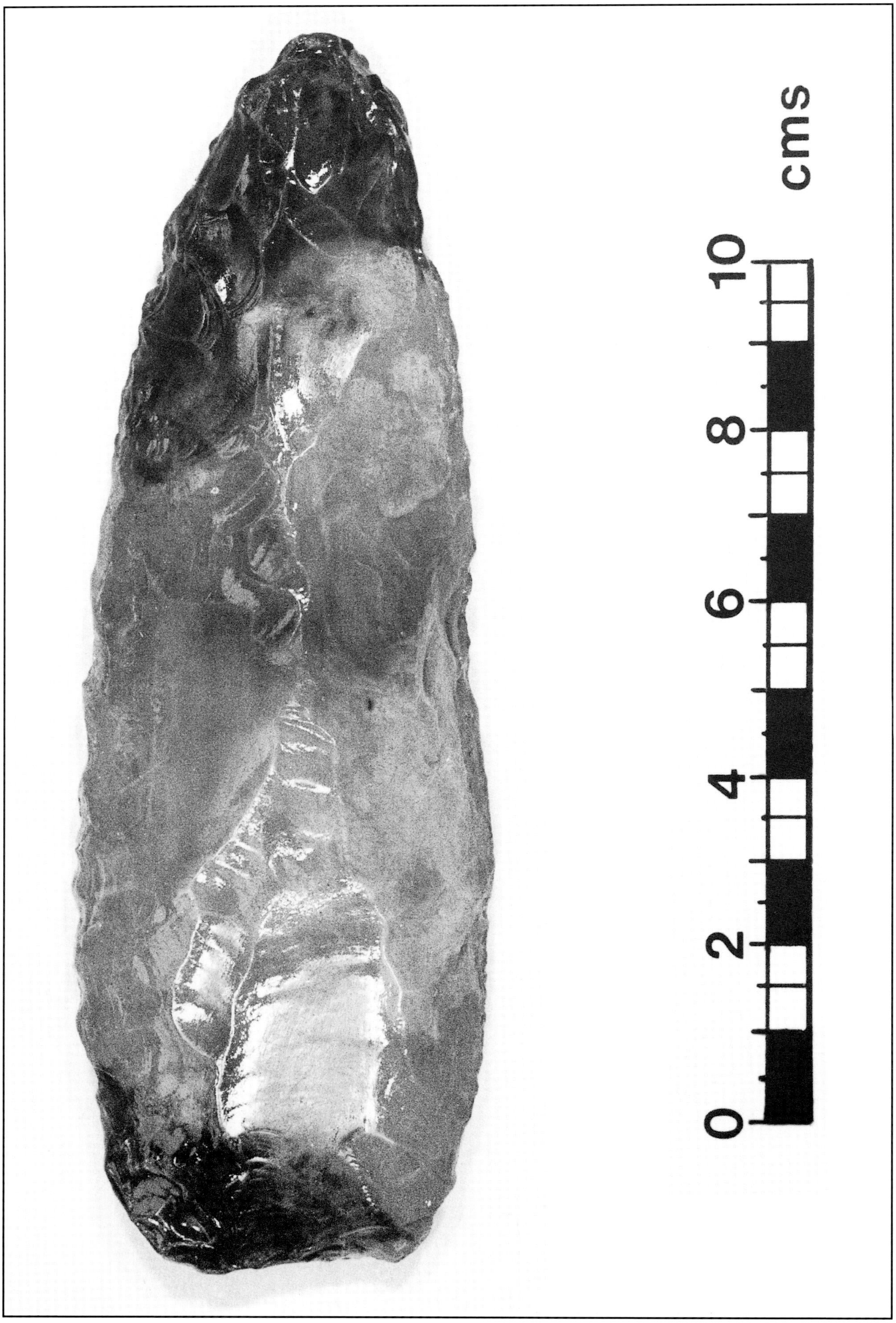

Illustration 19 - The Medlock flint adze. (Photograph of a resin replica: Barbara Booth).

Other Neolithic Finds

Green Withens Burnisher

SD 991165 1175 ft (358 metres) O.D.

This implement was found during the drought of 1976 on the bank of Green Withens Reservoir by Mr. H. E. Iredale, who presented it to Saddleworth Museum. It is made of a light coloured, almost white flint and has the appearance of a small axe with a narrow butt and a wide cutting edge. It is $2\frac{3}{4}$" (70 mm) long, $\frac{1}{2}$" (14 mm) thick and, at its cutting edge, $1\frac{3}{4}$" (45 mm) wide.

The edge is round and polished and in the opinion of T.G. Manby, may have been used or re-used for the polishing and rubbing of skins - in other words, for leather work. He considers it to be of Late Neolithic in date and that it may have started life as a true flint axe (Stonehouse, W. P. B. and Schofield, A.) [81] (see Illustration 20).

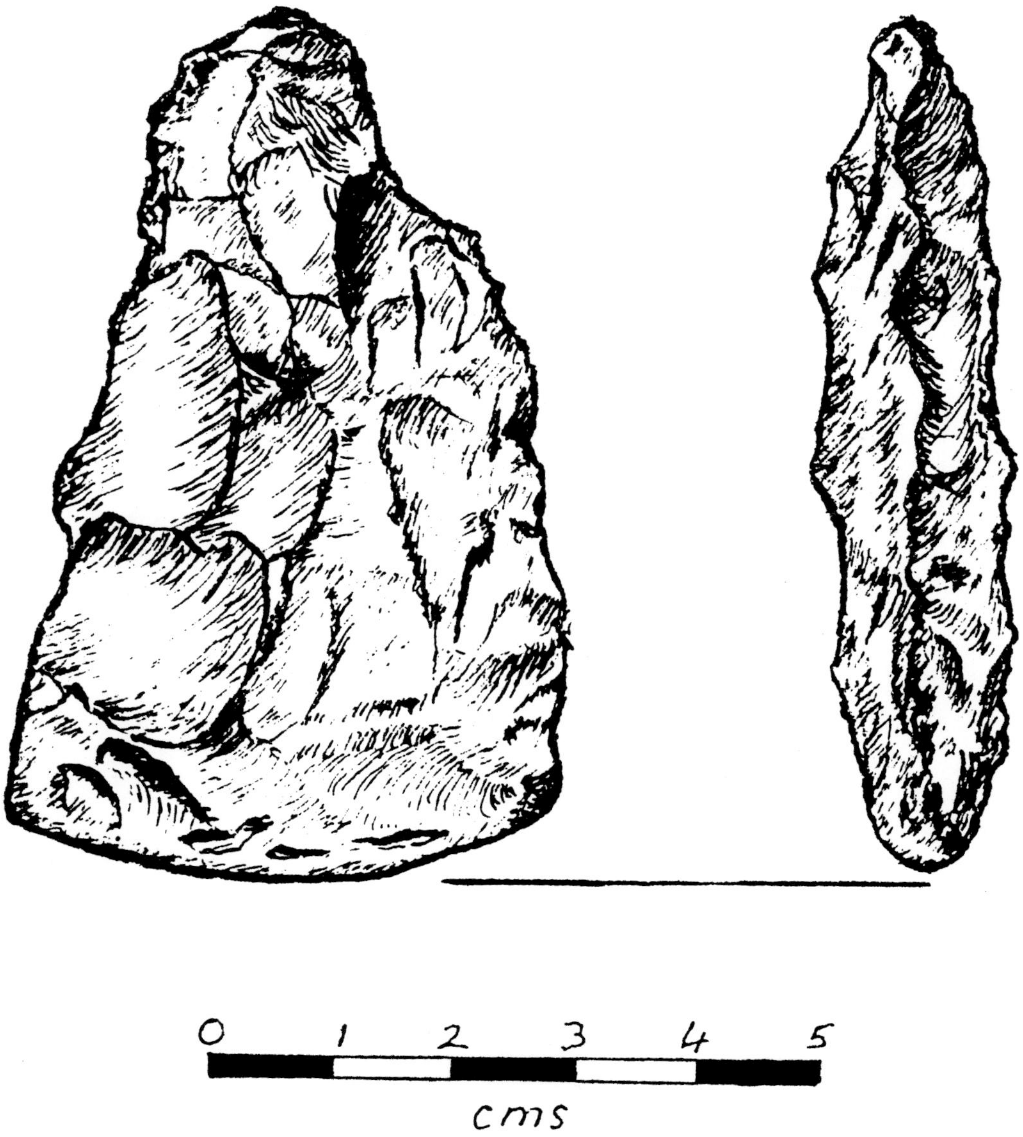

Illustration 20 - The Green Withens burnisher, found by H E Iredale. (Drawn by Alec Schofield and reproduced by kind permission of Phyllis Schofield). See Saddleworth Historical Society Bulletin, Vol 11, No 4. Reference [81].

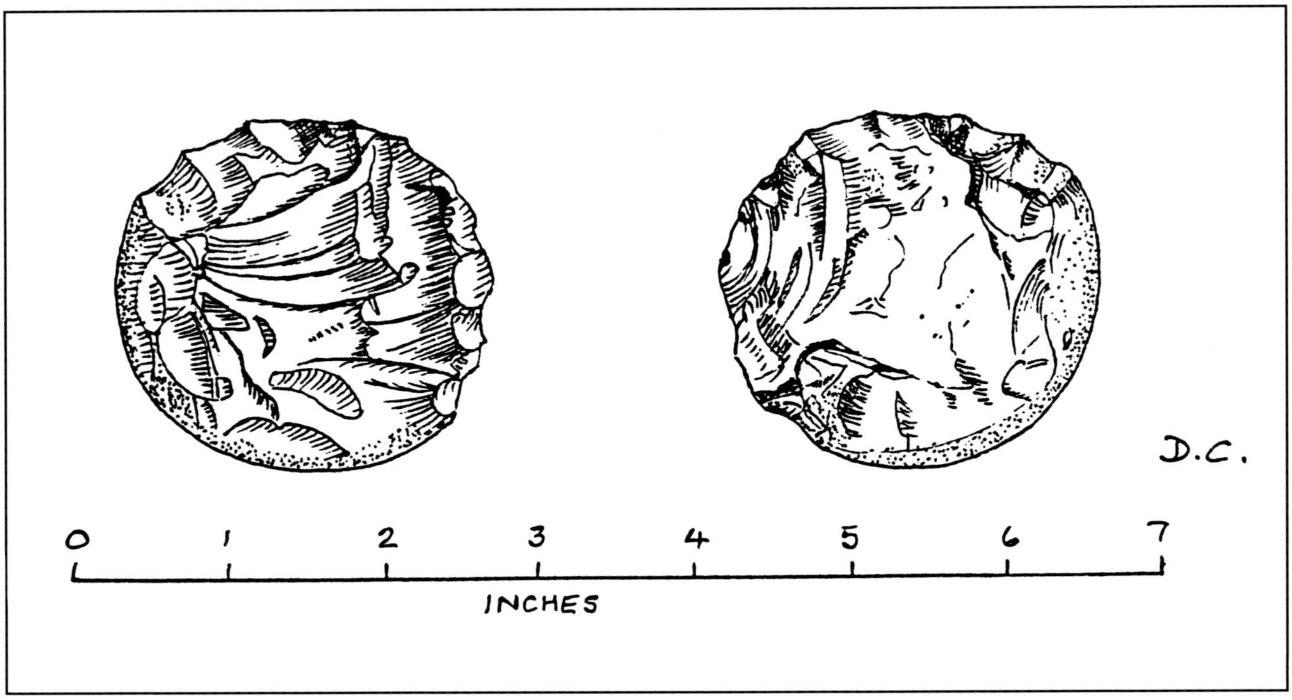

Illustration 21 - A polished discoidal flint knife found on Slatepit Moor, above Carrbrook, Mossley. Redrawn by D. Chadderton from J. P. Smith's photograph in Trans. Lancs. & Ches. Antiq. Soc., Vol 71, Fig XXXIII, Reference [53]. (By kind permission of the Lancashire and Cheshire Antiquarian Society).

The Slatepit Moor Polished Discoidal Flint Knife

SD 995007 1150 feet (350 metres) O. D.

Another Late Neolithic implement found in the locality is a polished discoidal flint knife found at a height of 350 metres on Slatepit Moor, on a large erosion patch on the northern edge of the moor overlooking Carr Brook, Mossley.

This is of grey flint and is flaked on both surfaces to make a thin disc, whose edge was then polished. It is of elegant workmanship, almost circular, 2.6" (66 mm) long, 2.4" (61mm) broad, with a maximum thickness of 0.4" (10mm). There is a cast of this in the Tolson Memorial Museum. (J. Davies, 1961) [53] (see Illustration 21). The J. Davies Collection is now lost.

A fragment of bifacially flaked edge ground Blade Knife of Later Neolithic date was found on Shore Moor, north of Rochdale and is in Manchester Museum, and an edge-polished flint chisel, found at Torside reservoir, Longdendale, by F. Hepworth of Stocksbridge, also of Grooved Ware date, 3500 -2500 B.C. is now in Sheffield City Museum (Manby, 1974) [52].

The finding of these examples of Late Neolithic implements in the district, together with transverse arrowheads on our moors, shows that man continued to exploit this neighbourhood in the Later Neolithic. This is confirmed by the excavation carried out by Stephen Poole at Piethorne Brook, Milnrow, just to the north of the Saddleworth boundary (S. Poole, 1986) [5]. This excavation will be described in greater detail in chapter three, but is relevant here in that it produced two fragmented leaf shaped arrowheads, and among 165 fragments of pottery, some fragments were identified by J. A. Gilks as an All-Over Corded Beaker, a type which is early in the Beaker series and may even be regarded as being of Later Neolithic Age. No other pottery of this kind has been found in the Central Pennines.

In 1994 a pottery fragment was found by Lee Cherry on the eroding surface of the southern edge of the gully which lies at the foot of the steepest slope of Pule Hill at SE 0316 1013, and thus on the side of the gully furthest from the summit. This was seen by T.G. Manby, who identified it as a rim fragment of the wall of a Peterborough Ware bowl or jar. There were the remains of one pit on the neck and two rows of finger and thumb impressions.

Lindley Moor [9]
SE 115192

A geophysical survey was carried out by GSB Prospection in order to identify the course of the Roman Road (Margary 712) which was thought to run across a proposed development site at Lindley Moor, Huddersfield. (OS Grid Reference: SE 115192). On the basis of the survey results, in 2000, two trenches measuring 65m by 4m and 30m by 3m and a larger open area were machine excavated and hand cleaned by Northern Archaeological Associates in order to identify the course of the road and to evaluate anomalies recorded by the survey.

The existence of the road could not be confirmed but a shallow pit containing sherds of Prehistoric pottery was excavated at the eastern end of the site. Examination of the sherds by T. G. Manby indicated that at least two vessels of late Neolithic Grooved Ware were present, and charcoal from the pit was dated to between 2470-2200 cal. B.C. (at 95% probability). The pottery represents a welcome addition to the limited number of Grooved Ware finds in the Central Pennines.

A carbonised hazelnut from a second, nearby small pit was dated to 7300 - 6750 cal. B.C. (at 95% probability), placing the feature firmly on the Mesolithic Period. A full report on the investigation, which discusses the significance of the features, is in preparation.

Pollen Analysis

Pollen analysis shows little forest clearance in the Central Pennines during the Early Neolithic, although Hicks S.P. (1972) [47] envisaged a minor intrusion onto the Sheffield moors around 3000 b.c. with, perhaps, a little growing of grain in temporary clearings. Bartley D.D. [21] found little evidence for Neolithic interference with the woodlands on Rishworth moor at an altitude of 410 metres (1300 feet). It seems that throughout this time the forest persisted up to a height of 365 metres (1200 feet) O.D. and that the local hills continued to be used for hunting as in Mesolithic times. Seasonal grazing of cattle probably took place, which would leave little trace in the archaeological record, apart from horn cores of the aurochs (*Bos primigenius*) surviving in the peat formations. An example of a large Bos horn, found by Stephen Poole was in Rochdale Museum.

An idealised section from the surface of the peat formation down to the sandy shale layer at Warcock Hill, above Marsden, showing stratification of remains, may be found in *Early Man in the District of Huddersfield*, Petch, J.A., Fig. 23, [37].

---

[9] *Information kindly contributed by T.G. Manby from the publication "Forum 2000", C.B.A. Yorkshire.*

Discussion

Neolithic man was certainly present in Saddleworth in both Early and in Later Neolithic times as is shown by the finds of axes and arrowheads.

The axes are found mainly in the valleys and low lying areas, but this is not quite so obvious in Saddleworth itself. The axes were, presumably, used mainly for the forest exploitation such as the cutting of leaf fodder.

The arrowheads have a different distribution, being found almost always on the moors, usually at altitudes of 1200 feet O.D. or more, and indicate the persistence of hunting on the lower edge of the open landscape/environment.

Barnes, in *Man and the Changing Landscape*, (1982, p.39) [1] has pointed out that arrowheads and axes in the Central Pennines have a contrasting distribution. The arrowheads are found mainly in the uplands, whereas the stone axes are usually found around the periphery of the uplands, often on the flanks of major valleys.

However in Saddleworth and its immediate surroundings, this is not true, and only three out of the nine axes mentioned in the list above were found below 800 ft O.D.

Settlements, where both axes and arrowheads may well be found together, together with evidence of flint knapping, and sherds of pottery, are very rare indeed, and of course the bones of domesticated or wild animals do not normally survive in the acid moorland soils and peats.

In the Central Pennines most of the axes originate from sources in Cumbria, but some come from North Wales, South Wales, Cornwall and even from Northern Ireland, (See reference [96]) so there must have been a complicated communication network. Trade routes have been postulated but are difficult to demonstrate. Note that the Standedge watershed is also the narrowest crossing point between the axe distribution areas each side of the Pennines.

Pollen analysis has shown only small clearings in the forest, which remained largely intact, which compares sharply with the situation in the Wolds of Yorkshire, the White Peak of Derbyshire, and the great chalklands of the south, where open land suitable for arable farming was created. Peat bog, probably initiated in Mesolithic times, persisted and spread.

The economy was probably a pastoral one with some movement onto the higher ground during the summer.

Hunting continued on the higher ground, as in Mesolithic times, and in fact it may have increased, as indicated by the scattered finds of arrowheads which relate to these late Neolithic times that are found in the gritstone Central Pennines (Manby, 1974,) [52].

This type of economy, shifting pastoral activity with hunting, probably persisted unchanged into Early Bronze Age times.

1 - Neolithic flint axe found by Lee Cherry, south of Readycon Dean Brook. (Photograph: Barbara Booth).

2 - Bronze Age V-notch amber bead found during the excavation of Jackson's Barrow in 1974. (Photograph: Barbara Booth) (3.6 times full size).

3 - Bronze Age arrowhead found near Abraham's Chair by James Holden. (Photograph: Barbara Booth) (2.8 times full size).

4 - Bronze Age looped palstave from Wall Green, Denshaw. (Photograph: Barbara Booth) (1.4 times full size).

5 - Bronze Age socketed spearhead from Piethorne Reservoir. (Photograph: Barbara Booth) (1.4 times full size).

6 - Castle Hill, Almondbury, Huddersfield. (Photograph: Barbara Booth).

7 - Torside Castle, Longdendale. (Photograph: Dr. W. P. B. Stonehouse).

8 - Dr. Pat Stonehouse working at one of his Pule Hill sites in 1984. The method Pat used was for each excavator to work on an individual square yard. (Photograph: Ken Booth).

9 - Excavation of Jackson's Barrow, 1974. David Chadderton at work, with Bleakhey Nook and Millstone Edge in the background. (Photograph: Barbara Booth).

CHAPTER THREE

Bronze Age

Earlier Bronze Age 1700 b.c. to 1300 b.c.
Later Bronze Age 1300 b.c. to 650 b.c.

The manufacture of objects made of copper, bronze and gold is the distinguishing feature of the Bronze Age. Copper is found in the British Isles in S.W. England, N. Wales, W. Scotland and S.W. Ireland. Copper is also found in small quantities in other places, and has indeed been found at Alderley Edge in Cheshire, where there is evidence of Bronze Age mining. Tin is mainly found in Cornwall. Bronze is an alloy of copper and tin[10] which requires skilled temperature control to make, a capacity well within the limits of the skilled potters who made fine ware such as Beakers. Lead was sometimes added in the Later Bronze Age as it made for an easier flow and the alloy formed at a lower temperature, but it was softer.

The Late New Stone Age merged almost imperceptibly into the Bronze Age, which is subdivided into an Earlier and a Later period. The Earlier Bronze Age is a time when the climate was particularly favourable and was a period of expansion into upland areas. The gritstone uplands of the Pennines show signs of this increase in population and activity by the presence of the burial mounds and ring cairns, by clearance cairns and by field systems, and the many chance finds of barbed and tanged arrowheads. More significantly, finds of scrapers and knives of Bronze Age type, which are occasionally associated with flint debris, indicate settlement. All this activity on the uplands seems

Illustration 22 - Drawings of Bronze Age pottery vessels. (Dr. W. P. B. Stonehouse).

to have come to an end with the Late Bronze Age, by which time the soil had become exhausted in an acidic soil environment, peat bog was extending to lower levels, and the climate had probably begun to deteriorate.

The barrows, mounds and cairns usually contain pottery vessels, described as Beakers, Food Vessels and Urns (see illustration 22).

'Beakers' are well made thin walled pottery vessels of tall striking shape and usually red in colour. The earlier examples date back to the New Stone Age, circa 2500 BC, and the late forms accompany a crouched inhumation beneath a round mound accompanied by other grave goods such as copper daggers, wrist guards, V-perforated buttons, double pointed awls, barbed and tanged arrowheads and stone battle axes.

'Food vessels' are thick walled, broader, heavier pots, which often accompany burials, which may be either inhumations or cremations. Another small vessel, called a pigmy cup or accessory vessel is associated with food vessels, but more often accompany collared urns.

Food Vessels, like the Beakers, accompany burials in the Southern Pennines and are concentrated in the Peak District, where more than fifty have been found on the limestone, but few on the nearby gritstone moors. Only eight possibilities have been found in the Central Pennines, but the most important site, Pule Hill, lies within two miles of the Castleshaw beaker find, just on the Marsden side of the Pennine watershed.

'Collared Urns' are large, heavy vessels and are widespread in the Central Pennines, generally on the fringes of the higher gritstone areas or in valleys (Barnes, 1982) [1].

The period of Beaker usage is associated with the emergence and spread of metal working across Western Europe, first of copper, and later of bronze, and was formerly considered to be the result of folk migrations by the 'Beaker People'. However, the fact that it was not associated with any new form of settlement, and that even the ritual monuments have predecessors of New Stone Age date, has suggested the idea that what really happened was the rapid spread of a prestigious packet of artifacts adopted by the aristocrats of a complicated society ripe for the development of metal work. Radiocarbon dating now shows that Beakers, Food Vessels and Collared Urns can be broadly contemporary and that they are found together in the Earlier Bronze Age.

The Beaker Folk, Food Vessel People and Urn Folk have all disappeared into the mist, and the three fold division of the Bronze Age into an Early, Middle and Late period has (except for consideration of metalwork) been replaced by a simple Earlier and Later Bronze Age - a decision based on social and technological changes. This suggests a very complicated society with different sections of the community being buried with different grave goods according to a different ritual. Early Beakers nearly always appear with warrior burials, but later Beakers often appear to accompany craftsmen.

---

[10]*Editor's Note: Early bronze contained about 90% copper and 10% tin; the higher the tin content, the harder the bronze.*

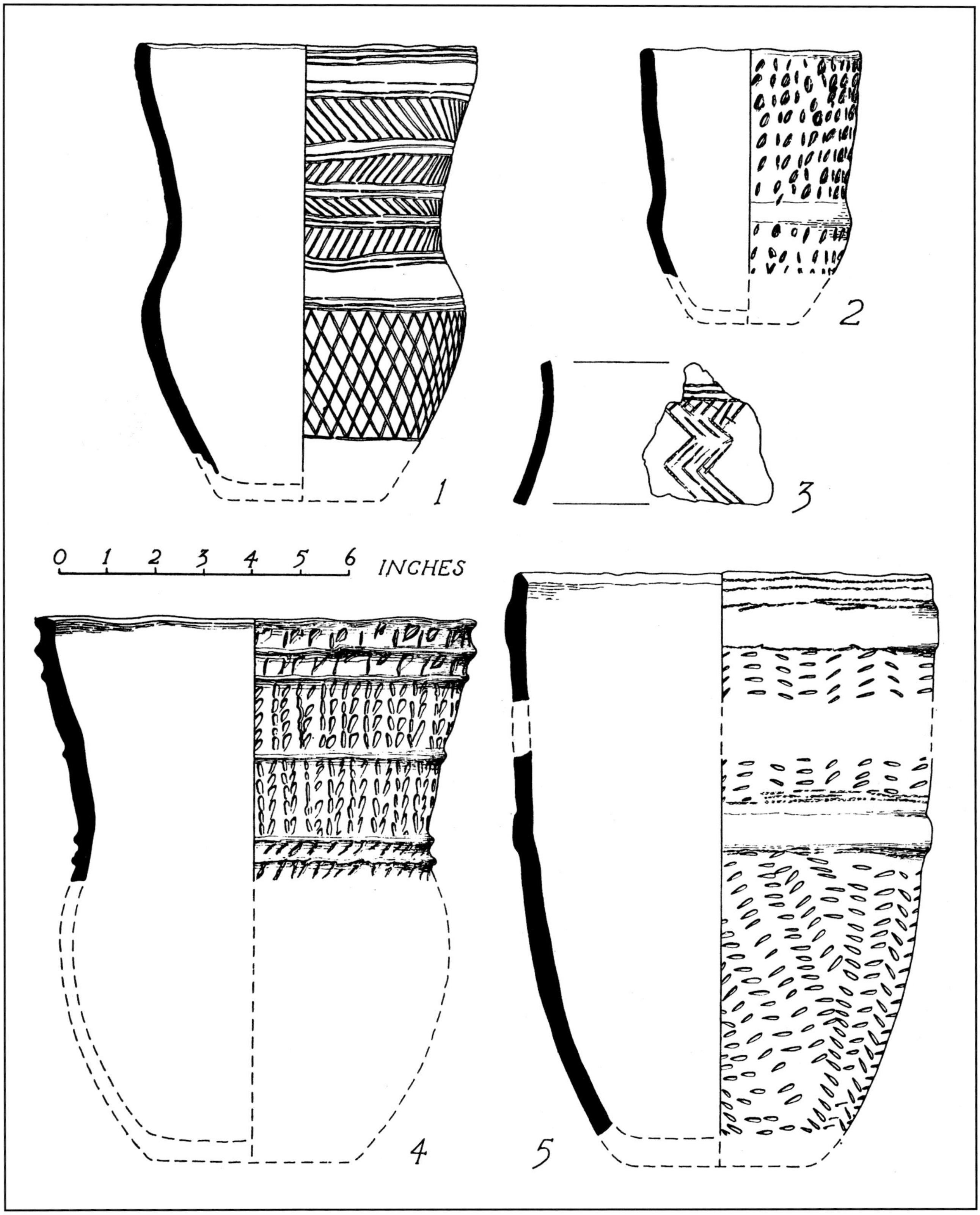

Illustration 23 - Drawing from the Castleshaw excavation report, of F. H. Thompson's reconstruction of beakers from sherds found in Trench 6. (Reproduced from Reference [3] by kind permission of Sheila M. Thomson and the Lancashire and Cheshire Antiquarian Society).

Local Evidence

Castleshaw
SD 99830967

Perhaps the most exciting and interesting Bronze Age discovery in Saddleworth is the finding of a pit beneath the floor of Castleshaw Roman Fort during the excavations of 1964 (Thompson. 1967) [3]. This was 21" in diameter and had been cut into the underlying rock to a depth of 15". It contained clean brown soil and some charcoal and was packed with 122 beaker sherds, from which five beaker vessels could be partially reconstructed. (See Illustration 23).

Beakers and Beaker burials across the Southern Pennines are fairly common on the limestone area of Derbyshire, but are very uncommon on the gritstone hills to the north. Barnes (1982) [1], only records seven possible occurrences in the Central Pennines, so this Castleshaw discovery was a tremendous find.

The five vessels are described by Clarke (1970) [4] as a characteristic selection from the Late Southern Beaker domestic array and included a giant storage beaker with rusticated decoration. One of the vessels is shown in Illustration 24. (A copy of a photograph of the reconstructed urn that is now Accession Number 1976.45 in the collection of The Manchester Museum).

The suggested date is 1550 B.C. (Thompson 1967) [3]. This find indicated that there may have been a Beaker period Bronze Age settlement in the Castleshaw Valley at this date.

Ragstone
SD 99331190

Ragstone is a small but prominent rock outcrop situated at 1200 feet (365 metres) O.D. about 1¼ miles (2 km) to the North West of Castleshaw Fort on the north side of the A640 (the outcrop is marked on Illustration 5, p.21).

A beautifully made flint dagger was found in three broken pieces by Norman Gartside, a twelve-year-old schoolboy, in 1924 at Ragstone. Two of these pieces were found on the 3rd of January but it was not until the 18th April that his perseverance was rewarded by the finding of the last piece (Petch, 1937) [37]. A colour photograph of the dagger, which is 140mm long by 50mm wide, appears on the front cover of this book.

Daggers such as these are probably imitations in flint of metal prototypes and are often found accompanying beaker burials.

Flint daggers accompanying later Beaker Burials in the Peak District are rare in the gritstone areas, but Ragstone is one of the cluster of Flint Dagger sites found along the western side of the Pennine watershed. This dagger was presented to Saddleworth Museum by its finder Norman Gartside shortly before his death.

Illustration 24 - Urn No. 1 in Illustration 23, reconstructed from sherds found in the trench at Castleshaw (from a photocopy of a pre-1969 photograph of the urn, Accession Number 1976.45, and reproduced by courtesy of The Manchester Museum).

Jackson's Barrow [11]

SE 0020 0905

A little over half a mile to the east of Castleshaw Fort, a suspected Bronze Age round barrow was excavated by Saddleworth Historical Society in 1974. In the first season the South West Quadrant was excavated and produced four finds of significance:-

1) an unfinished V-notch amber bead of a 'Beaker Folk' type,
2) a fragment of a Roman unguent bottle, greenish in colour, and similar in type to a piece found during the 1908-11 excavations of the Castleshaw Roman Forts. (Find Book No. G5),
3) a sherd of pottery, possibly from a beaker,
4) a piece of vitrified material, which would suggest that burning had taken place within the confines of the barrow mound.

The V-notch amber bead is illustrated on Colour Plate 2. Bernard Barnes commented on this bead (a private communication to Ken Booth). 'Exactly like a bead on a necklace of 219 beads (140+ amber) illustrated in Fig. 888, J. R. Mortimore, *Forty Years' Researches in British and Saxon Burial Mounds of East Yorkshire*, London, 1905. From Barrow No. C44 in the Driffield Group.'

The central area of the mound was natural, but a cavity in the core of the rock contained blue clay deposits.

The site was vandalised after the first season and no further excavation has taken place.

No burials were found, but bearing in mind that only one quadrant was excavated, it is impossible to speculate what may be awaiting discovery in the remainder of the mound. It has been suggested that the barrow was a natural mound, which had been utilised as a burial place. The Roman glass may point to a visit or use by the occupants of Castleshaw Roman Forts in antiquity. (See Colour Plate 9 for a general view of the barrow).

Piethorne Brook, Milnrow

SD 97451370

In addition to the finds at Castleshaw, fragments of four beakers and of two collared vessels were found on a site excavated by Stephen Poole just to the north of the Saddleworth boundary (Poole, 1986) [5]. They were accompanied by nineteen scrapers, two Neolithic arrowheads (broken) two jet spacer beads and part of a shale ring.

One of the beakers was an 'All-Over-Cord' beaker, which is early in the Beaker series. The site itself lies on a flat, south-west facing spur about 20 metres from and eight metres above the present stream at a height of 1000 feet (305 metres) O.D. A favoured spot, it was sheltered from the north wind by Windy Hill, and was utilised in Mesolithic, Neolithic and Early Bronze Age times. The presence of four beakers and two collared urns might suggest that this was a burial place, although the siting, almost on the valley floor, is unusual. Some sixty small pieces of bone (so small as to be unidentifiable) in a rather large hearth suggested to the excavator that the hearth 'represents not only the clamp in which pottery was found, but also a cremation pyre'. However, the excavator also noted the large number of scrapers and scraper spalls, and 'a number of pebbles showing polish and wear

---

[11] *Editor's Note: This section, on Jackson's Barrow, was kindly rewritten, at Dr Stonehouse's request, by Ken Booth.*

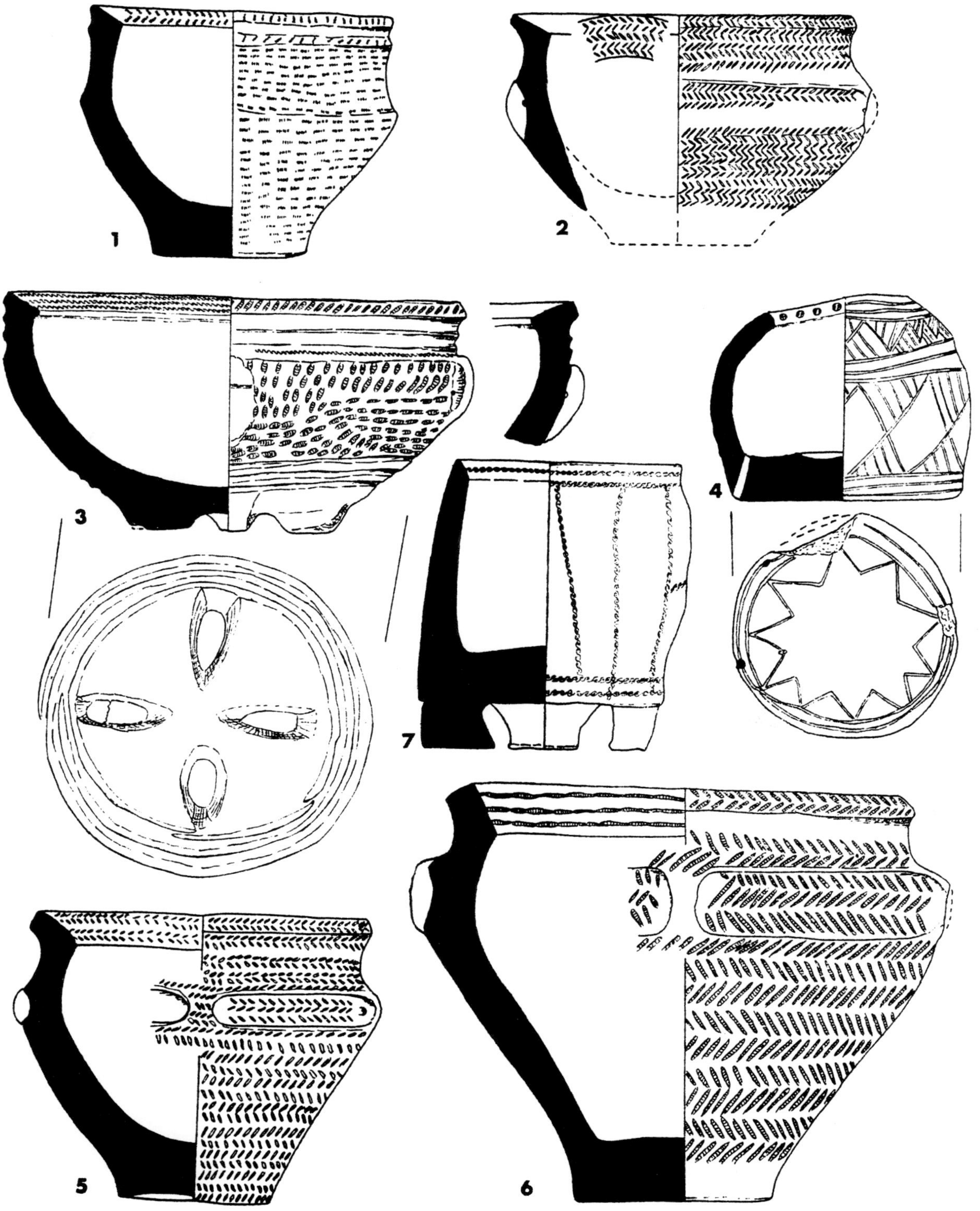

Bronze Age Pottery from Pule Hill, Marsden 1–4; Ferry Fryston 5; Halifax 6; Pickering 7.

Illustration 25 - Drawings of Bronze Age pottery from Pule Hill (Taken from the Journal of the Yorkshire Archaeological Society, Vol 62, pp 273-282, Reference 9, by kind permission of T. G. Manby and the Hon. Joint Editors of the Yorkshire Archaeological Journal).

patterns, and a series of carefully placed slabs' - which 'strongly suggest that skin or leather working was taking place on site'.

This would imply that the site was a settlement site, and this view is reinforced by the finding of further Bronze Age flint work on the adjoining spurs upstream.

Pule Hill, Marsden
SE 03211040

Pule Hill is a prominent hill, 1400 feet (426 metres) high, which from the west and south appears as a steep-sided cone, rising 200 feet above a moorland plateau. Here, two Marsden men, Firth Fell and George Marsden, started to dig in 1896 after the finding of an arrowhead near the summit. They unearthed two very decayed crouched inhumations and nearby two Food Vessels lying on their sides and containing calcined bones and animal matter.

One of the vessels contained a barbed and tanged arrowhead. Two further Food Vessels and a large Accessory Cup with two perforations in the base were also found. (See Illustration 25).

An excavation was carried out by a committee of the Yorkshire Archaeological Society in 1899 (Clarke, E K, 1902) [8] and found no trace of a barrow, but discovered three cavities in the underlying rock 3 feet long, 2 feet wide, containing bone, charcoal and flints. The vessels can be seen in the Tolson Memorial Museum, Huddersfield, and are considered by T.G. Manby (1969) [9], to have affinities with East Yorkshire, rather than with the South. One of the Food Vessels is somewhat unusual in being footed. Footed bowls are rare types. Pygmy vessels are small decorated vessels of unknown function and often have holes or slits in their sides or base and are sometimes called incense cups. Manby suggests that one of the Food Vessels closely resembles another found on Harland Edge in North Derbyshire which has been dated to 1490 ±150 b.c. The Accessory Cup (See illustration 25, No. 4) has been dated to around 1400 B.C. by Manby, who considered that the whole assemblage might not have been buried at the same time. The absence of a mound might be due to it having eroded on this very exposed summit or possibly this was what is known as a flat cemetery (Manby, T. G. 1969) [9].

(The fourth food vessel appears to have been lost - it was kept by F. Fell).

Brown Hill, Saddleworth
SD 99800650

Brown Hill is a small knoll near where Saddleworth Railway Station used to be.

In May 1844 quarrymen discovered two urns and a pebble macehead - together with some calcined bones and charcoal. The accounts are somewhat vague, but it appears that the bones were those of a child, and according to Ammon Wrigley (1911) [10] who is quoting from Bradbury, J., *Saddleworth Sketches* (1871) [11], the coroner was notified and arrangements made for holding an inquest. However, George Shaw of Uppermill, who was also an antiquarian as well as an architect, realised that the finds were those of a prehistoric burial.

Wrigley (1911) quotes two letters written by George Shaw, one in May (that is in the same month that the finds were made) in which he says he visited the site and that the two urns lay about 4 feet

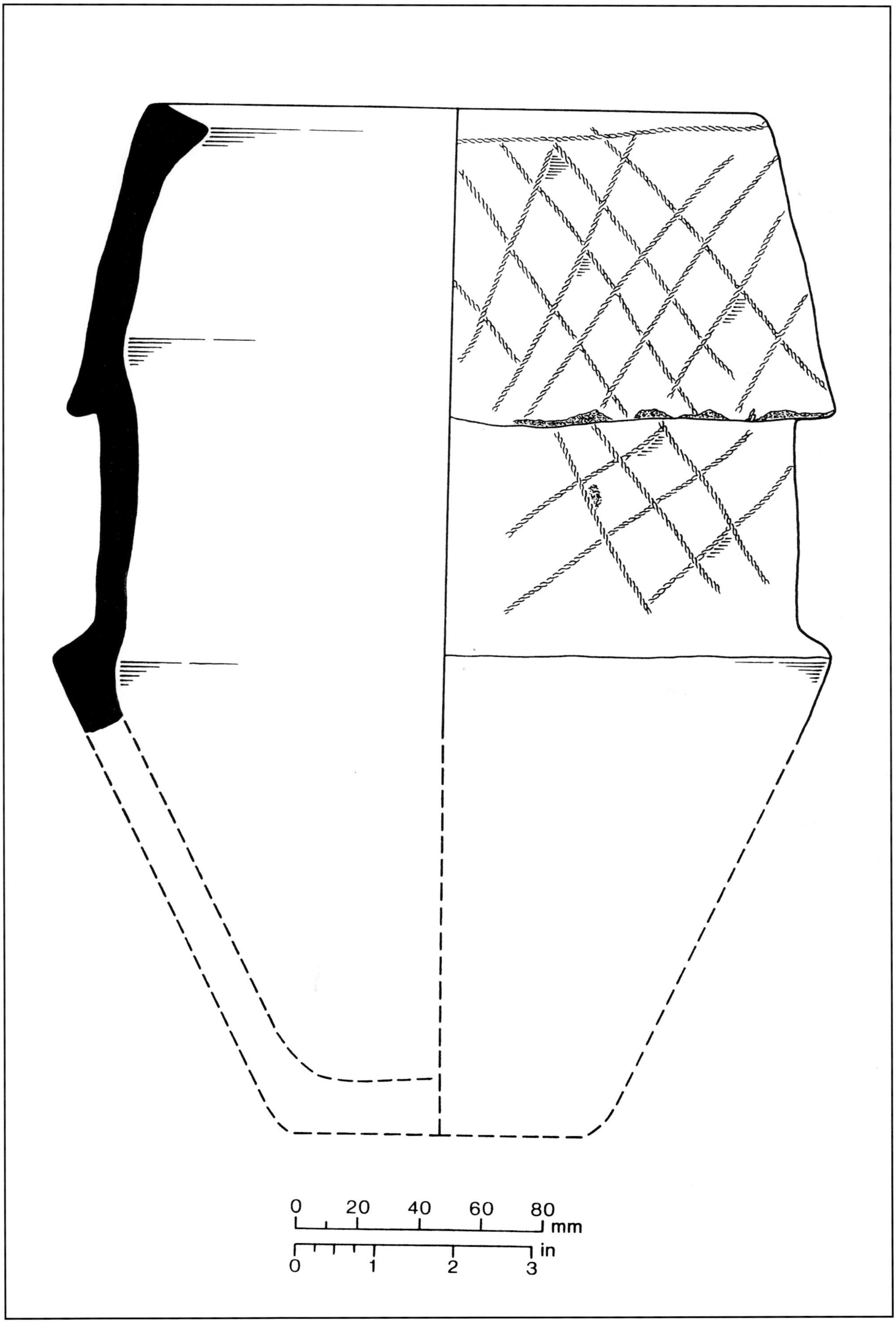

Illustration 26 - Earlier Bronze Age collared urn from Brownhill, Saddleworth. (Drawn by J.A.Gilks).

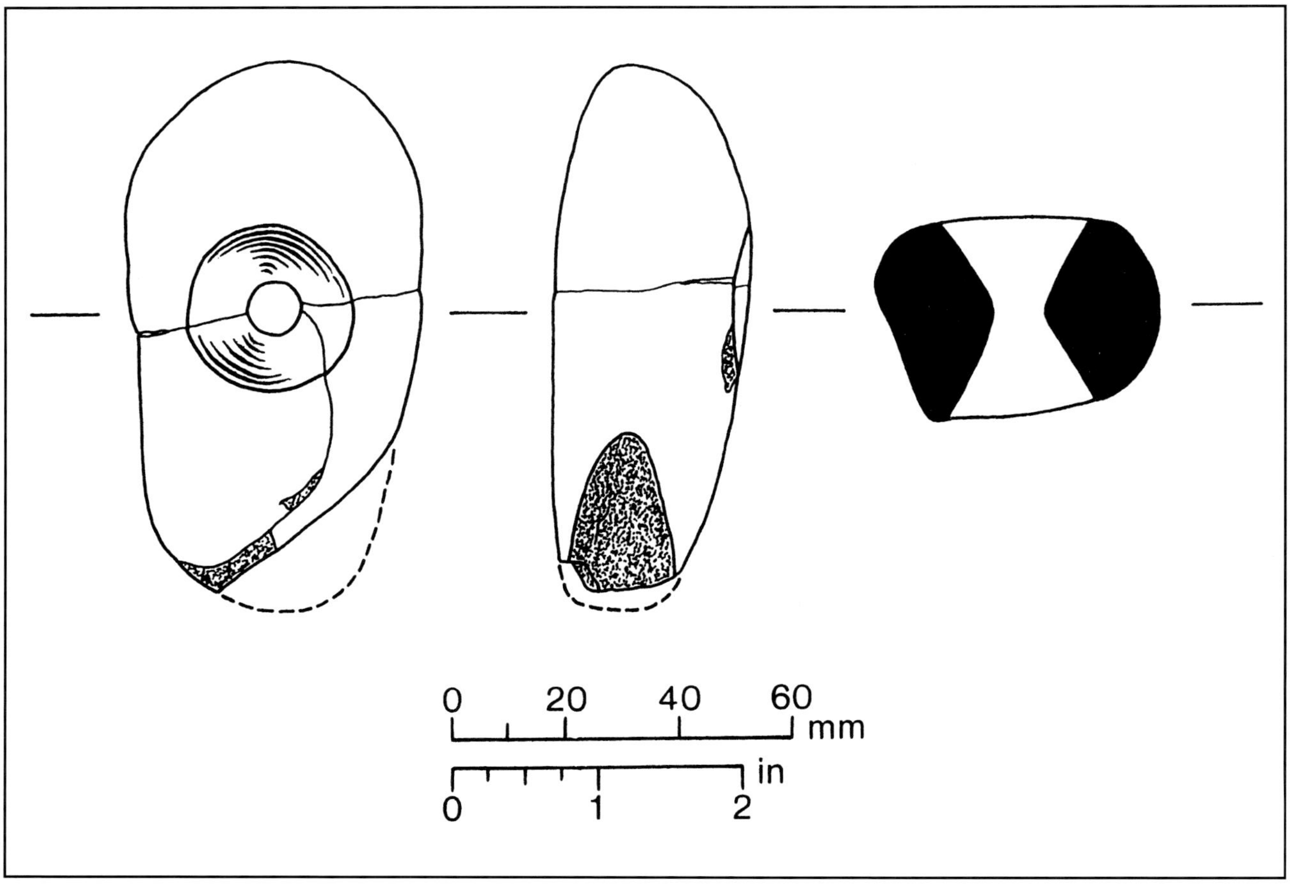

Illustration 27 - Earlier Bronze Age pebble macehead from Brownhill. (Drawn by J. A. Gilks).

apart and some 18 or 20" from the surface. The other letter dated 17th June states that the urns were 4' 6" below the surface. Gilks (1977) [7] suggests that these figures can be reconciled if the second reading is from the top of the covering mound and not from the land surface.*

Fragments of one urn and the pebble macehead are now in the Tolson Museum in Huddersfield. The function of stone maceheads is unknown and when discovered as chance finds are difficult to date as they occur not only in the Bronze Age, but also in the New Stone Age and Middle Stone Age (see Illustrations 26 and 27).

The 'urns' appear to have been decorated on the collar with a network of lozenges made with a twisted cord. Collared Urns are by far the commonest sort of vessel found in the Central Pennines and are usually associated with cremation burials. They are large, 8 to 20" or more in height, and are often thick and clumsy in appearance but can be well made and thin walled. In Derbyshire they occur, in contrast to Beaker and Food Vessels, on the gritstones rather than on limestone. Barnes (1982) [1], describes occurrences in the Central Pennines.

It is impossible to be certain that the Brown Hill burials were in fact covered by a burial mound or cairn, but such 'barrows' are fairly numerous in the Central Pennines and a map showing their distribution is given in B Barnes (1982) [1].

**Editor's Note: Bradbury, J., in 'Saddleworth Sketches' (1871) [11] p.207, writes 'Subsequently another stone celt, of a flat adze-like shape, was found near the same spot, and preserved with the former one.' (Personal communication from Ken Booth).*

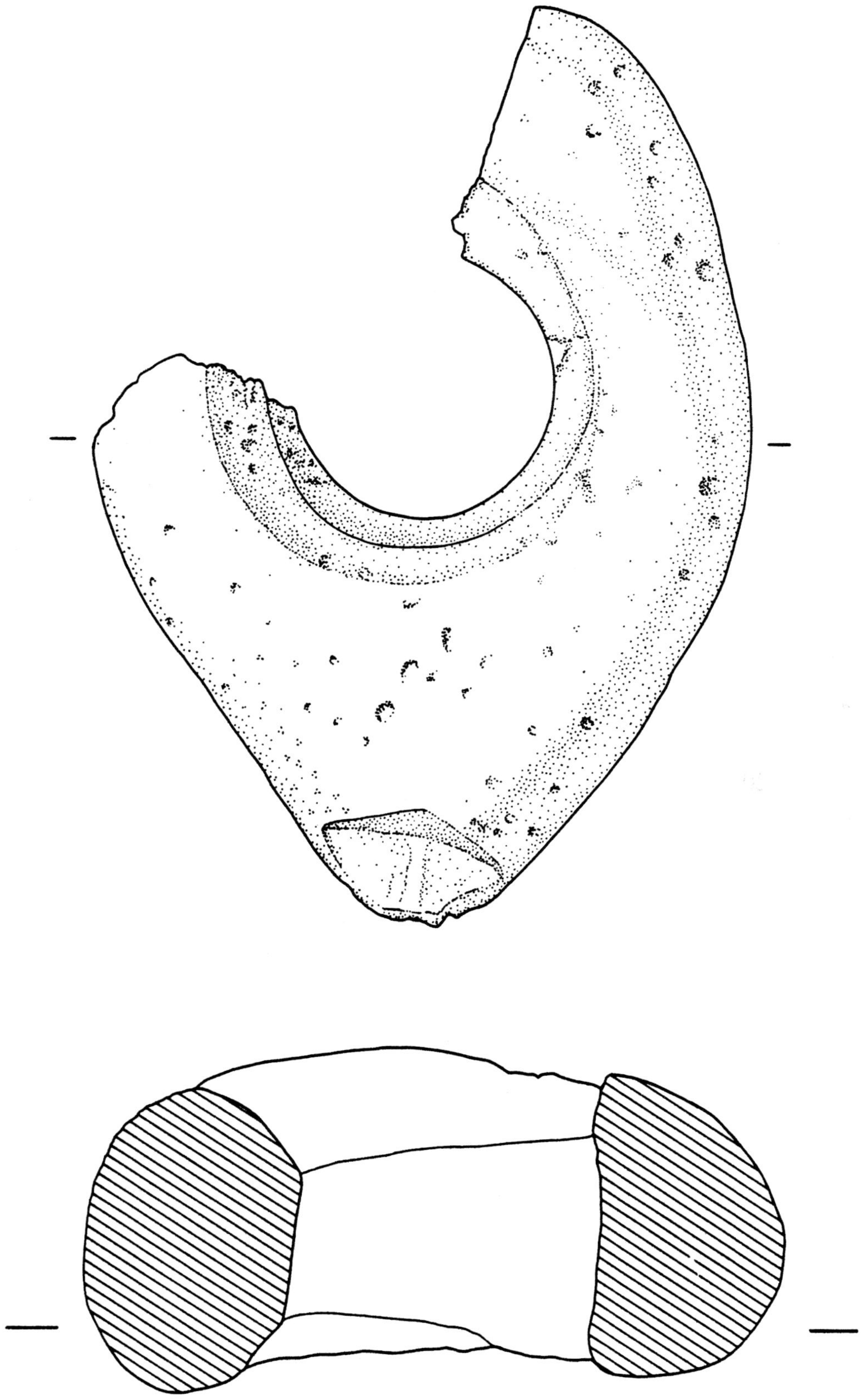

Illustration 28 - Stone macehead from Werneth Low (Reproduced from 'Tameside Before 1066', by kind permission of Dr. M. Nevell and Tameside M.B.C.) (3 times full size).

Illustration 29 - Dowry Castle, on the south east side of the Buckstones Road, overlooking Dowry Reservoir, above Denshaw. Now considered to be a natural landslip feature. (Photograph: David Chadderton).

Stone Macehead, Werneth Low
(Exact find spot unknown)

The butt end of this axe was broken in antiquity, possibly as a result of the over-large socket which is 56 mm (2.2") in diameter. It is made of millstone grit and is 189 mm (7.3") long by 132 mm (5.2" wide). The axe end has been damaged quite recently. The exact find spot is unknown but there is a possibility that it originated from the barrow behind Werneth Low (see Nevell, M., 1991) [84].

The place name 'low' often indicates the presence of a tumulus and Bateman (1861) [12] listed some 250 examples in Derbyshire and Staffordshire. Ammon Wrigley (1911) [10] gives some Saddleworth examples of placenames containing the word 'low' such as Lowgate, Warlow, Back o'th' Low, Shelderslow, but none of these has produced evidence of a barrow.

Broadhead Noddle, Saddleworth
SD 99171037

Ammon Wrigley [10] identified two barrows near the summit of Broadhead Noddle, a prominent rounded hill which dominates the upper of the two reservoirs in the Castleshaw valley. One was a bell shaped mound on the eastern shoulder of the hill, which was sixty feet in circumference and three feet high. Excavation revealed 'strong evidence of fire' and also 'a substance resembling white chalk' which Professor Boyd Dawkin identified as a kind of white marl. Wrigley also discovered a smaller mound a few yards to the west with a depression 'suggesting that it had been opened and rifled at some period'. It is difficult to identify either of these mounds at the present time.

Hill Top, Saddleworth
SD 98010745

In a meadow near the summit of Knott Hill, Delph, at a height of 1000 feet (305 metres) O.D., Wrigley (1911) [10] described a 'large and well defined ring mound', 15 yards in diameter and 3 feet high. Wrigley dug five small trenches, but his only finds were 'pieces of charcoal and fragments of burnt stone'.

The site was subsequently surveyed by Saddleworth Historical Society but unfortunately permission to make a full excavation was not obtained, although enough work was done to confirm that this was a man made circular structure, probably a ring work or the remains of a barrow. (The site is now a scheduled Ancient Monument).

Ring Works

'Ring works' are circular structures with low embankments of earth or stones, often without an entrance, enclosing a central space. The circles are on average 35 feet in diameter and enclose multiple burials. Barnes (1982) [1] tables twenty-nine in the Central Pennines, one of which, Blackheath, Todmorden, contained at least eight collared urns and four pygmy accessory cups.

There are no stone circles in Saddleworth and only a few in the Central Pennines, but there are many in Derbyshire where the stones are usually placed just within a low embankment, a famous example being that of the Nine Ladies stone circle on Stanton Moor.

Having discussed some sites within and just outside Saddleworth, which include Castleshaw with its Beakers; Pule Hill with Food Vessels and Brown Hill with Collared Urns, it remains to be said that this area has produced nothing in the way of the bucket, barrel and globular urns of Deverel-Rimbury tradition. These were originally thought to belong to the Late Bronze Age but are now firmly rooted in the Early Bronze Age.

Little Barrows, Diggle, Saddleworth
Grid Reference (of Fairbanks Farm) SE 008074

Joseph Bradbury in his *Saddleworth Sketches* (1871) [11] states that 'On the Fairbanks property in Harropdale a tumulus may still be seen which has evidently given its name to the field in which it is situated' - 'Little Barrows', and adds that it was opened a number of years ago but that 'no one at the present time appears to know with what result'.

Ammon Wrigley (1911) [10] was unable to confirm these findings and noted that the Little Barrow enclosure is the site of a rather extensive sand pit and that 'if ever a tumulus had existed (it) had been carelessly destroyed by pitmen'.

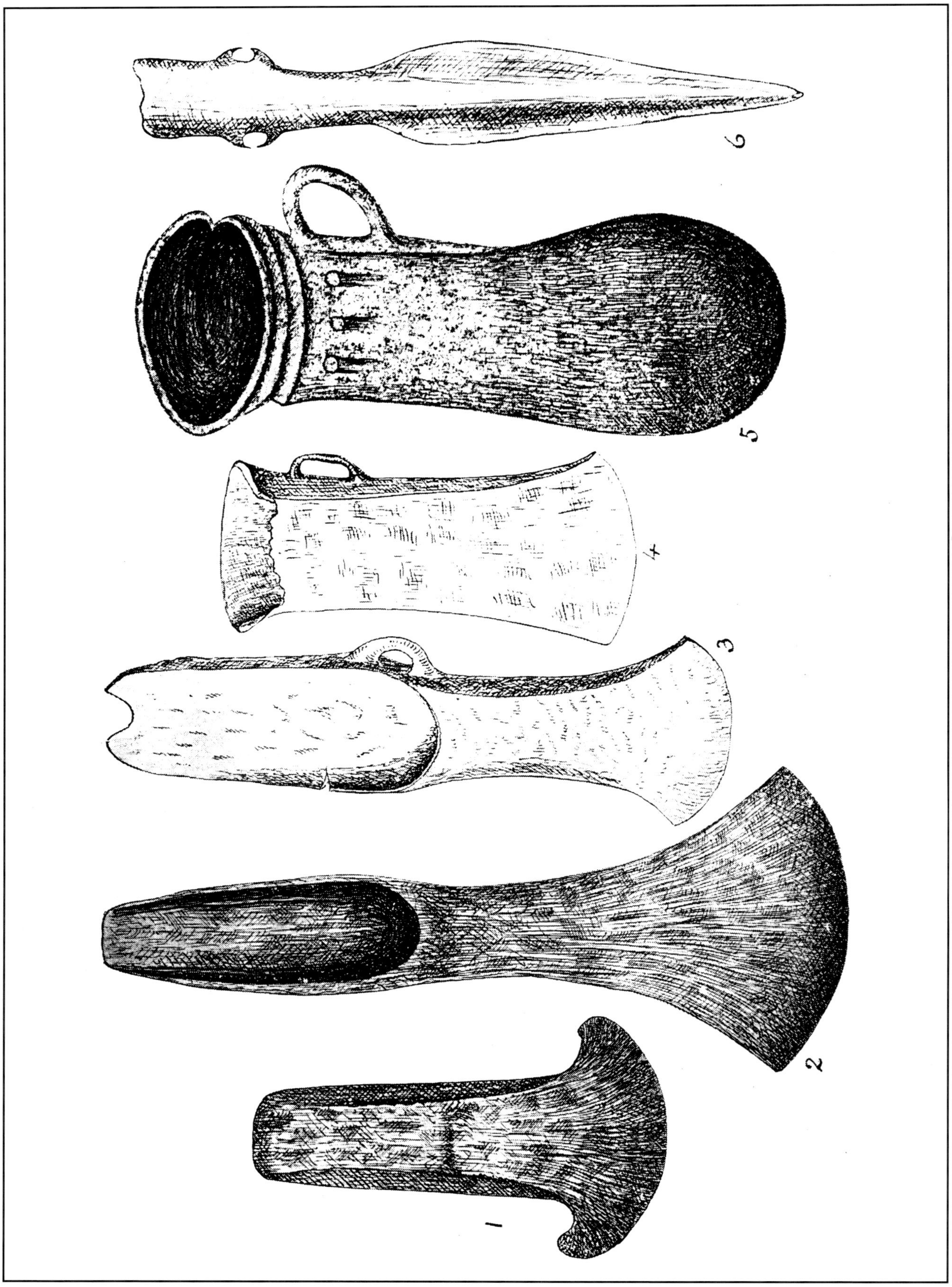

Illustration 30 - Drawing of the development of Bronze Age axes. No. 1 is the Arreton flanged axe from Rishworth, No. 2 is the palstave with a stop ridge from Greenfield, No. 3 is a looped palstave from Sowerby, No. 4 is a typical square socketed axe, No. 5 is Ammon Wrigley's drawing of a Late Bronze Age socketed axe, considered to be the one found at Castleshaw, pre 1771. No. 6 is a Bronze Age spear head from Cartworth Moor. (Reproduced from 'Early Man in the District of Huddersfield', by J. A. Petch, by kind permission of the Kirklees Community History Service at Tolson Memorial Museum, Huddersfield).

Ringstone Edge Moor, Barkisland
SE 04451825

This is of course, is not in Saddleworth but it is only 8 kilometres from the Saddleworth border. It has produced a number of monuments of possible Bronze age date, including a ring work, 88 feet in diameter, now much damaged, seven small mounds or clearance cairns, the largest 4 metres in diameter which may possibly be burial structures, and a number of circular paved areas visible in the floor of Ringstone Edge reservoir when the water level is low which may be the remains of hut circles. The ring work is said to have produced a cinerary urn.

A.T. Longbotham carried out an excavation in 1905, which found 20 feet in from the north eastern edge of the circle "five separate interments". These consisted of small areas about the size of "one's clenched fist" of dark greasy material.

An urn was found by A.T. Longbotham lying to the south west of the centre of the circle, encased on two sides by upright stones with a flat stone on top (Watson, G. G., [58], p.94, Lunn, N., [20], Longbotham, A.T., [79]).

Beacon Hill, Barkisland
SE 0450 1850

There is a round cairn on the northern edge of Ringstone Moor. Longbothom records an awl from it.

Dowry Castle, Denshaw
SD 990113

This unusual mound lies on the south east side of the Buckstones road (A640) from Denshaw to Huddersfield, overlooking Dowry reservoir. (See the map, Illustration 5.) Its striking pyramidal shape has led to it being considered to be a prehistoric barrow and Joseph Bradbury (*Saddleworth Sketches*, 1871) [11] wrote 'It is said that chests of gold and other treasure was buried deep beneath this mound" and "it is probable that the 'treasures' are the bronze instruments of some ancient British chief who was here interred -'.

Ammon Wrigley (1911) [10] recognised that the mound is 'an eccentric natural formation' and continues 'I have proved (this) by repeated excavations at various parts of the slope, finding in each instance a perfectly regular stratification of shale'. Ammon Wrigley, with his usual common sense, has hit the nail on the head. This is a natural feature, the result of a landslip. (See Illustration 29).

Lowhouse, Milnrow
SD 95061837

A cist (a box shaped burial structure made of stone slabs) contained in a Barrow, was found at Lowhouse in 1899. A cremation and a stone axe hammer were found. The urn was plain, 8" (203 mm) high and 8" (203 mm) diameter. The urn was destroyed together with its contents. (See later, p77, for description of the axe hammer) (Barnes, App.2, 172) [1].

Finds:

Metalwork

In discussing Bronze Age metalwork, the old tripartite division into Early, Middle and Late Bronze Age continues to be observed.

The Central Pennines, though not as rich as the Peak District, have, nevertheless, produced over 70 find spots (Barnes, 1982) [1]. Most of these are chance finds, and many are not well provenanced. Bronze axes form a typological sequence, starting with flat axes, and progressing through flanged axes to palstaves and eventually to socketed axes. (See Illustration 30).

Flat axes and flanged axes belong to the Early Bronze Age; palstaves, (Illustration 30, No.2) which have flanges and a stop ridge, to the Middle Bronze Age and socketed axes (Illustration 30, No.5) to the Late Bronze Age. It is worth noting that examples from all three 'Ages' have been found in Saddleworth or just outside its borders.

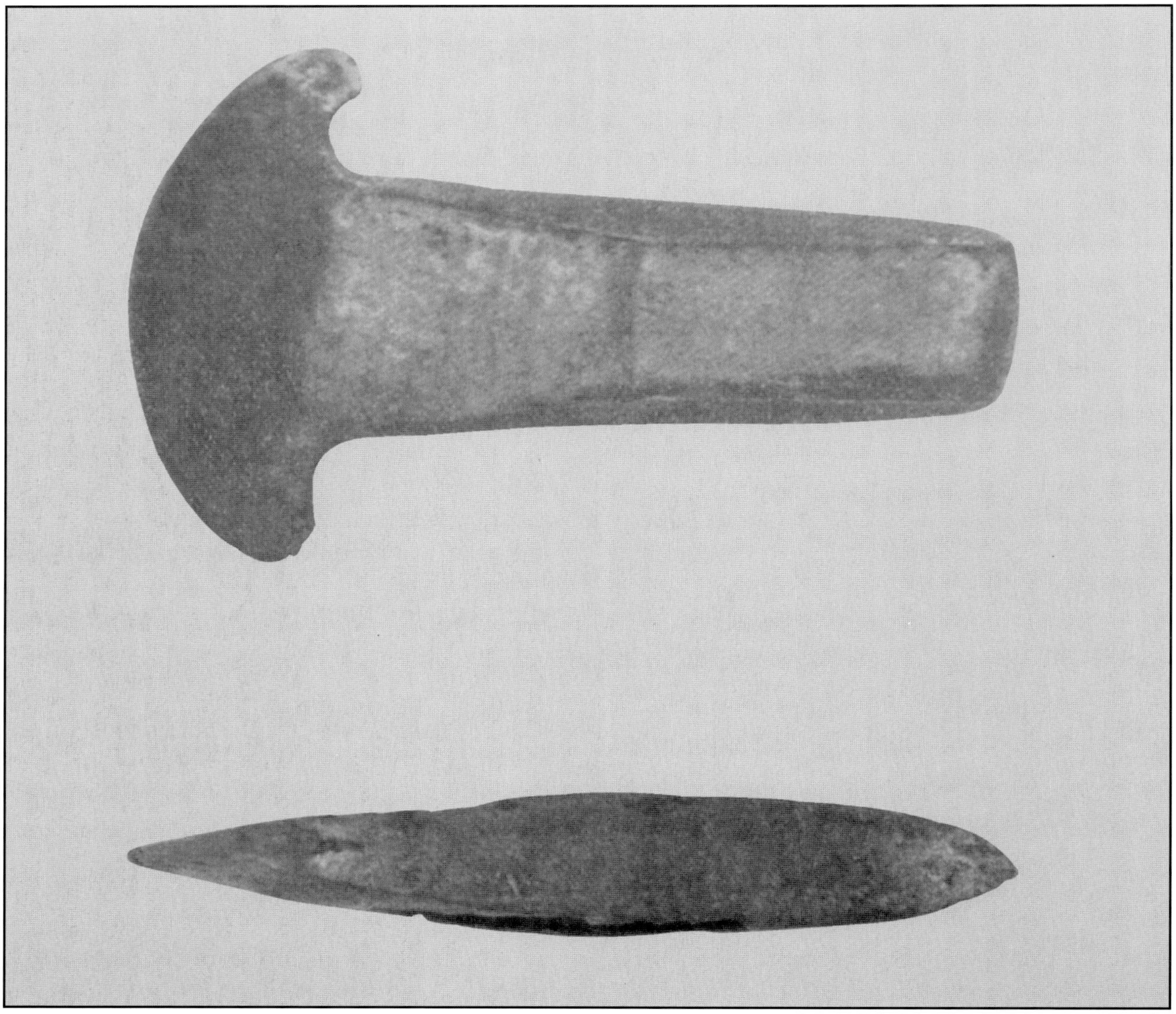

Illustration 31 - Ammon Wrigley's illustration of The Rishworth Moor flanged axe. (Reproduced from 'Saddleworth, Its Prehistoric Remains', by kind permission of Christine Seville and Ruth E Greenwood). (The illustrations are full size).

Arreton Axes

Rishworth Moor
SD 0116

A flanged axe of Arreton type was found high up on Booth Moor, Rishworth, not far from the Saddleworth boundary. In private possession, it is illustrated by Petch (1924) [37], and Wrigley (1911) [10], Plate C. (See Illustration 31). Rochdale Museum preserves a cast. Length 5", width of blade, $2\frac{1}{2}$".

Arreton type axes belong to the Early Bronze Age and are named after a hoard found in the Isle of Wight and occur mainly in South East England and along the south coast.

Palstaves

These are flanged axes with a well developed stop ridge. Three palstaves, all chance finds, have been found in this area - two within Saddleworth itself and one just over the border on Crompton Moor. These belong to the Middle Bronze Age, and an account of these is given below.

Spring Grove, Greenfield
SD 999042

This was found in 1860 - 61 on the site of the old Co-operative Stores, Chew Valley Road, and had a plain blade and convex flanges. Wrigley (1911) [10] illustrates the palstave, (Plate B) as do Davey, P. J. and Forster E. (1975) [24] (see Illustration 32). There is a cast in the Rochdale Museum (Barnes 1982, App. 2, 129) [1]. Length $6\frac{3}{4}$" (171mm), greatest width of blade: $2\frac{3}{4}$" (70mm).

Wall Green, Denshaw
SD 9710

This 'Transitional type palstave' (Wallington type) was found in 1932, eighteen inches from the surface, during the digging of a trench on the north bank of the River Tame. It is looped, $6\frac{1}{2}$" (165mm) long, $1\frac{1}{2}$" (38mm) wide at the cutting edge, with a stop ridge $3\frac{1}{2}$" (90mm) from the anterior end. It is in private possession but there are casts in Tolson Museum, Rochdale Museum and Saddleworth Museum and it is illustrated in Saddleworth Historical Society Bulletin Vol 12, No 2, 1982. Such axes must have been almost mass made and yet have considerable beauty. (See Colour Plate 4).

Crompton Moor, above Crompton Fold, Oldham
SD 965103

A third palstave, also of Transitional type, was found just outside Saddleworth on Crompton Moor by G. Radford. $5\frac{3}{8}$" (143mm) long, $1\frac{7}{8}$" (48mm) wide, it is in private possession but there is a cast in Rochdale Museum, and is illustrated by Davey and Forster, [24].

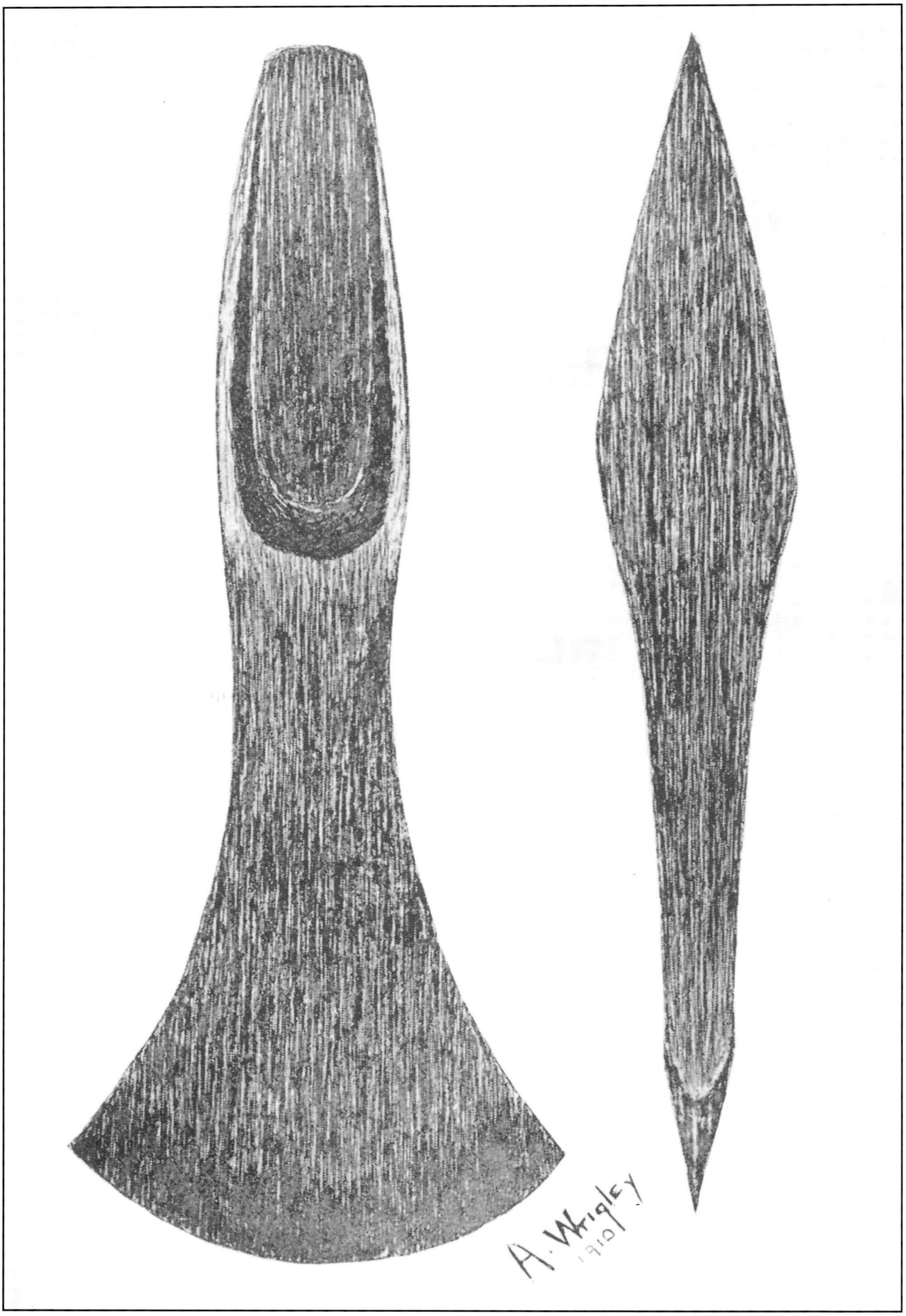

Illustration 32 - Ammon Wrigley's drawing of the Spring Grove palstave, Greenfield. (Reproduced from 'Saddleworth, Its Prehistoric Remains', by kind permission of Christine Seville and Ruth E Greenwood). (1.3 times full size).

Dean Clough, near Denshaw
SD 9812

This is a bronze dagger, mentioned by Petch (1924) [37], which is said to have been found in Dean Clough and was in Oldham Museum in 1924 (Barnes 1982) [1].

Piethorne, near Milnrow
SD 9612

A socketed spearhead, $6\frac{3}{8}$" (162mm) long, with lunate openings, found by the late G. Radford at Piethorne, Milnrow. Held in Saddleworth Museum. (See Colour Plate 5).

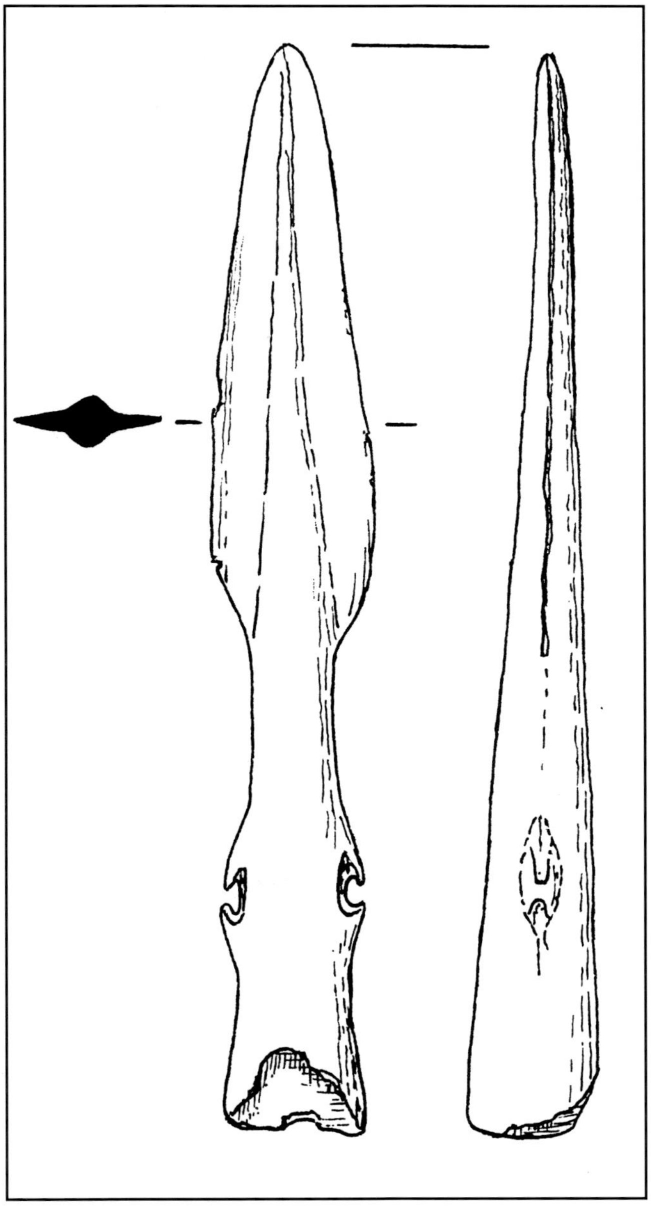

Illustration 33 - Drawing of the Cartworth Moor Bronze Spearhead found in 1811. (Actual Size). Original in Tolson Memorial Museum. (Drawing kindly provided by T. G. Manby).

Thornley, between Grotton and Mossley
SD 967037

Part of a rapier or spearhead-rapier was found in 1900 at Thornley in the valley between Quick Edge and Brown Edge, 'near the old track coming over Quick'. This was 14" (356mm) long, tapering from $1\frac{3}{4}$" (44mm) to a point. This looks like the blade of a very long spearhead. (Andrew, S., 1901) [72].

Cartworth Moor, Holmfirth
SE 1305

A small side-looped bronze spearhead with side loops broken, the edge of the socket damaged and the blade edge chipped was found during peat digging in 1811. The spearhead is 5.6 inches (142 mm) long and has a dark green patina. (Petch, J.A., [37], p. 55, and Barnes, B. [1], App. 2., 354. and orig. in Moorhouse, *Hist and Topog. of the Parish of Kirkburton etc.*, Huddersfield, 1861). Accession No. 60.13.47 in the Tolson Memorial Museum). See Illustration 33.

A similar spearhead was found in 1994/5 at Sowerby, (South of Sowerby Bridge). (Private communication from T.G.Manby).

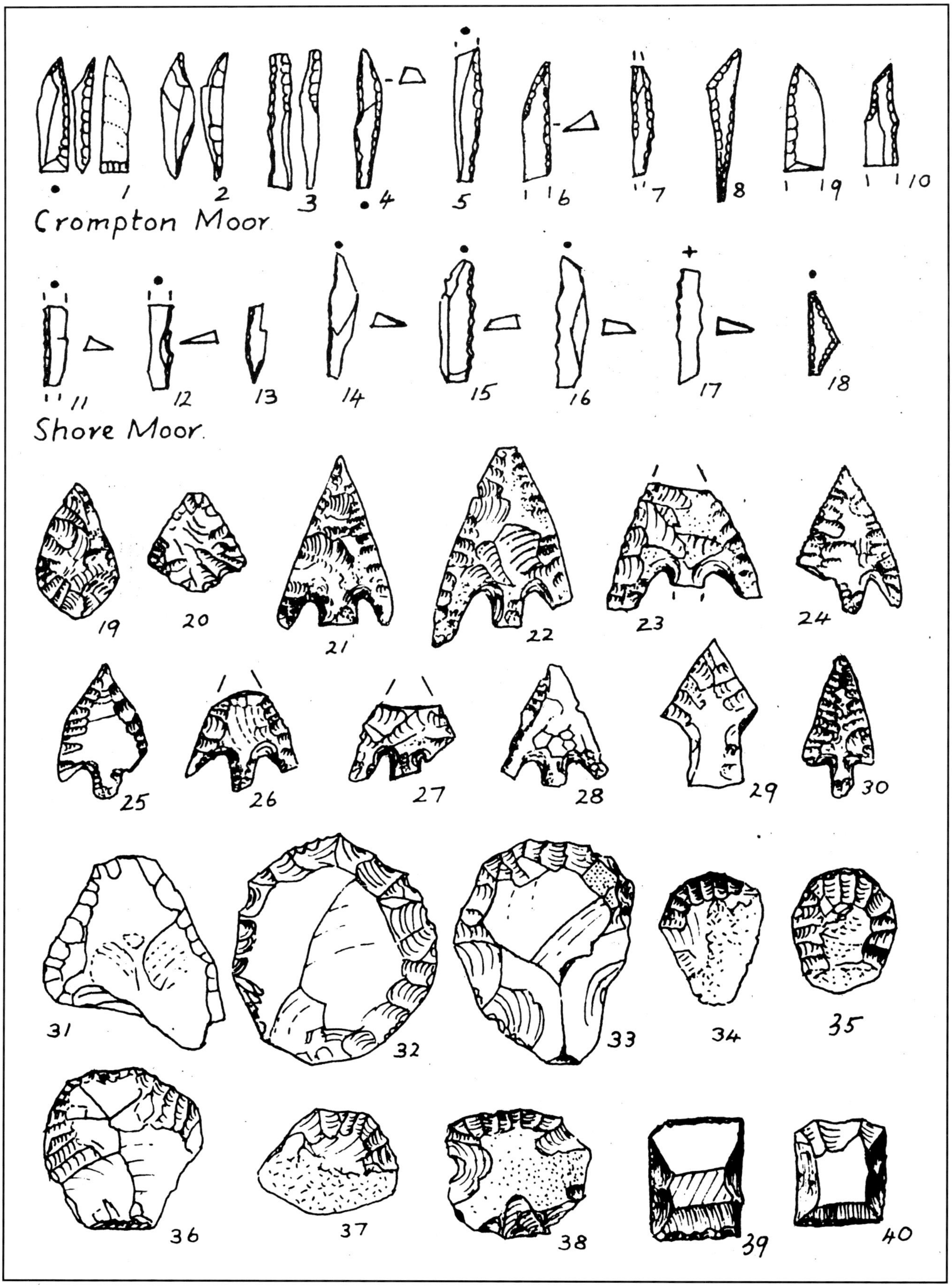

Illustration 34 - From the Thomas Hill collection: 19 and 20 are Neolithic arrowheads from Crompton Moor, 21 to 30 are barbed and tanged Bronze Age arrowheads, again from Crompton Moor apart from 24 and 25, which came from Windy Hill. 31 is an unusual flint, possibly of Neolithic or Beaker age, 32 to 38 are Bronze Age scrapers, all from Crompton Moor except 38 which came from Piethorne. Note that 39 and 40 are 17th to 19th Century flintlock gun- flints. (Drawing by Dr. W.P.B. Stonehouse, reproduced from Saddleworth Historical Society Bulletin, Vol.12, No.2. Reference [95]).

Stonework

The Brown Hill and the Werneth Low maceheads have already been mentioned. (See Illustrations 27 and 28.) Another pebble macehead made of quartzite, $2\frac{5}{8}$" (67mm) long and $1\frac{1}{2}$" (38mm) wide, with an hour glass perforation was found at Badger Slacks (O.S. Grid Reference SD 998121) near the Saddleworth - Marsden boundary by Dr. H. Colley March in the late 19th century, and is illustrated by Wrigley [10] (Plate K). A flint knife was found in the vicinity but both are now lost. (Barnes 1982, Appendix 2-113) [1].

An axe-hammer was found in Ramsclough, Slackcote, (Barnes, App 2, 127) [1] which was socketed, but the hole for the wooden shaft not bored right through (Petch 1924, p.40) [37], and another, 6.4" (163mm) long, 3.6" (91mm) wide and 2.5" (64mm) thick, was found within a cist (a box shaped burial structure made of stone slabs) contained in a barrow, now destroyed, was found at Lowhouse, Milnrow (Barnes, App. 2 172) [1].

The stone axe hammer was contained, together with cremated bones, in an urn, and is in Rochdale Museum.

Flint Types

The flint dagger found at Ragstone has already been described. Such daggers are plainly imitations of bronze tools and display excellent technique. They are chiefly known from burial contexts (S. Pierpoint. 1981) [18].

Barbed and tanged arrowheads have been found in large numbers as isolated finds on the moors. These come in different sizes and shapes, some obviously utilitarian, others, usually larger, so carefully and beautifully made that they appear to be 'prestige objects', not really to be used in the hunt. These are sometimes called 'Breton' or 'Armorican' arrowheads. The 'Armorican' arrowheads have obliquely cut barbs which are longer than the tang, the 'Breton' or 'Corrygar' types have square barbs and the base of the arrowhead is convex in plan. (Green, H.S., 1980) [73].

The examples shown in Illustration 34 come from a collection made by Mr Thomas Hill, of Mount Sorrell, Dobcross, in the early years of the 20th century, and have been loaned to Saddleworth Museum by his grandson, Mr S. Lawrence of Bamford, Rochdale, [95].

The first two, numbered 19 and 20, are of course Neolithic, and come from Crompton Moor. All the rest except Nos. 24 and 25, which came from Windy Hill, Littleborough, were also found on Crompton Moor.

Another fine Bronze Age arrowhead was found on the north side of Warlow Pike, near Abraham's Chair (SD 9902) by James Holden, of Friezland Lane, Greenfield, in 1953, along with two pieces of worked flint. (See Colour Plate 3).

Small round scrapers, characteristic of the Bronze Age, also occur, sometimes tending to concentrate together, as for example on Crompton Moor or Worlow, which lies near Marsden, above Mount Road, and not infrequently in association with plano-convex knives (slug knives) which in section are flat on one side and convex on the other so that they have a 'slug-like' appearance. 'Slug' knives occur in both the Late Neolithic and the Bronze Age.

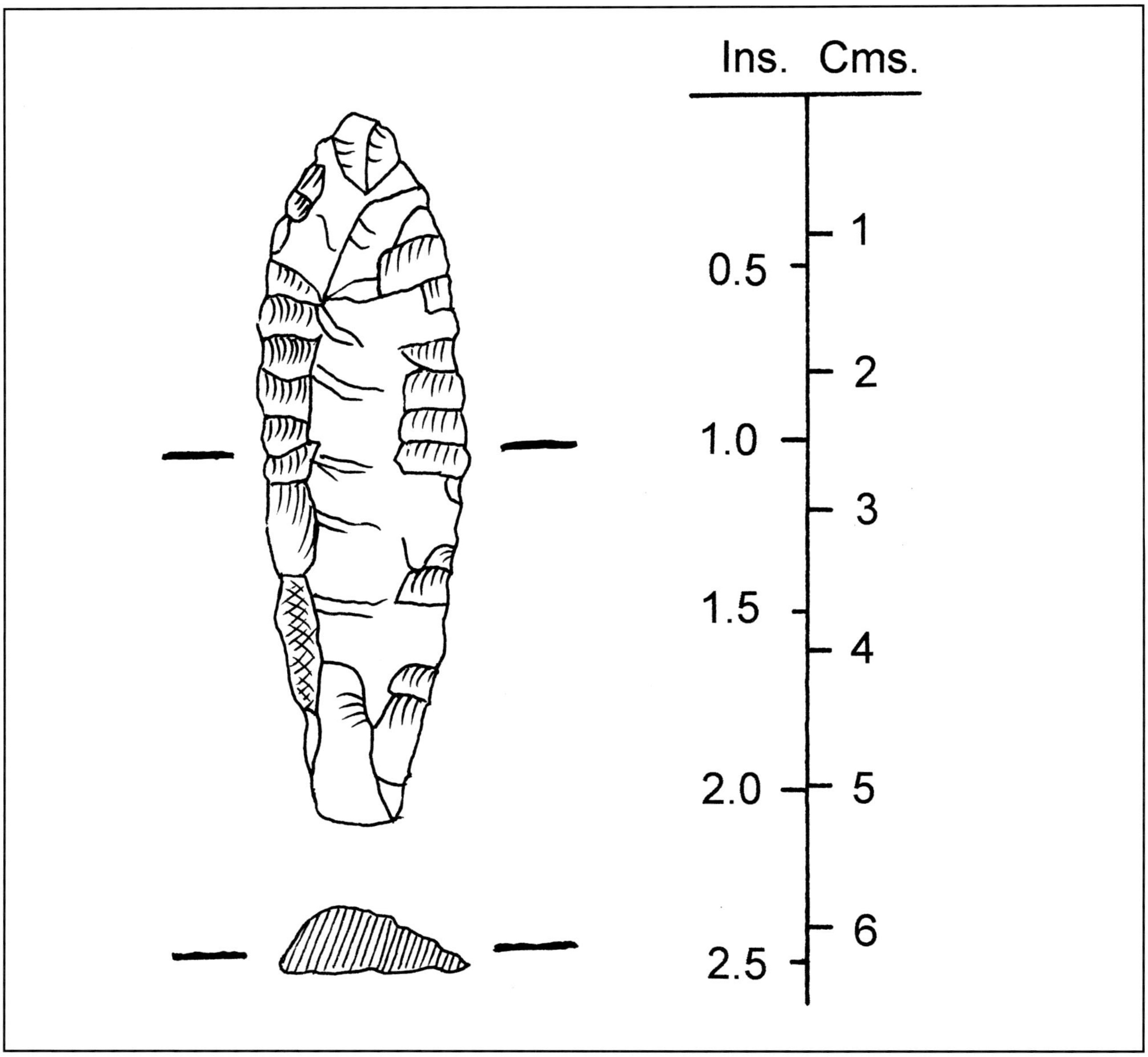

Illustration 35 - A plano-convex cross section flint 'slug knife'. Note the cross section shown below the main drawing. (Redrawn from an illustration of a slug knife found in the Yorkshire Wolds and reproduced by kind permission of T. G. Manby).

The round scrapers numbered 34, 35 and 37 in Illustration 34 may well be Bronze Age examples.

A drawing of the typical form of a slug knife (or a plano-convex knife) is shown in illustration 35.

The finding of barbed and tanged hunting arrowheads, slug knives and small round scrapers reasonably close to each other in some places suggests the possibility that there was some degree of exploitation of the uplands in Bronze Age times that went beyond just hunting.

This point will be considered in greater detail below.

Particularly prolific areas for Bronze Age finds of this type include - Crompton Moor, Pule Hill Slades, Worlow (Marsden) and Hind Hill (Marsden). These are all at an altitude of about 1000-1200 feet, but similar sites have been found in Wharfedale near the river and in the Saddleworth area and locally at Gilbert's Island, in the Wessenden Valley, near Marsden. This is an island that appears in the highest reservoir when the water level is very low (Stonehouse, 1982) [83].

The only excavation carried out on a Pennine site of this period is that of Piethorne Brook, described earlier (Poole, 1986) [5]. This produced no less than 405 pieces of waste flint, showing that flint working was carried out on the site.

Jet Ornaments

Jet beads were found at Piethorne Brook (Poole, 1986) [5] and jet studs from Castle Dean, Rishworth. (Tolson Memorial Museum).

Field Systems

Stone clearance cairns, linear banks and enclosures have been found in a number of upland areas and in some cases have been proved by excavation to be Bronze Age in date. In the Pennines, the most extensive upland area is that of the 'East Moors' of the Peak District - the moorland area near Sheffield. No evidence for such features has, as yet, been found in the Saddleworth area apart from some field clearance near Holmfirth, but it is worth noting that Cowling (1946) [16] identified some thirty Late New Stone Age - Bronze Age sites in Mid-Wharfedale (this includes Ilkley Moor), mainly on the hills.

Pollens

The pollen evidence suggests widespread forest clearance in nearly all upland areas during the Early Bronze Age but is less marked in this part of the Central Pennines where Bartley [21] found that the forest gave way only slowly to heather and cotton grass on Rishworth Moor. Here, a slight clearance phase was dated to 2060 ±100 b.c. Following these clearances there seems to have been an extension of blanket bog and Barnes (1982) [1] says, quoting Birks, 1965 [22] that 'by the end of the Bronze Age the upland plateaux were dominated by extending peat bog or heath, while the upper slopes below the peat line had an open discontinuous tree cover. The lower slopes and parts of the lowlands were probably grassland, especially where the better, well drained soils occured, as is suggested by some lowland pollen diagrams'.

The Later Bronze Age

A startling change occured about 1300 B.C. affecting every aspect of life. From this time onwards very few barrows were built and there were no more stone circles or ring works. Pottery styles change - the Beakers, Food Vessels and Urns all disappeared to be replaced by new forms. Metal technology changed. Some stone made objects such as axe-hammers disappeared. Barbed and tanged arrowheads probably persisted, possibly even into Iron Age times, but there seems to have been a general retreat from the uplands and it is noticeable that the late bronzes found in our area are merely chance finds in the valleys.

These later bronzes range from transitional palstaves that may date from as early as 1200 B.C. to socketed axes, which were not made until after 850 B.C. A socketed axe was found at Castleshaw pre 1771. When found it contained remains of an original wooden haft. (Whittaker, 1771 [15], and

Wrigley, 1911 [10].) A drawing of the socketed axe thought by Ammon Wrigley to be the one found at Castleshaw is shown in Illustration 30, No.5.

Hill top settlements began to appear, one example being Mam Tor near Castleton in Derbyshire, where at a height of 1600 feet (487 metres), platforms have been found on which timber huts had been constructed, which gave radiocarbon dates of 1130 ± 115 b.c. and 1180 ±132 b.c.

By 1100 b.c. there is clear evidence that the climate had deteriorated and this may have been an important factor leading to change.

Discussion

It is extremely difficult to understand the Bronze Age because settlement sites are so few and also because the finds are usually so badly provenanced.

The Earlier Bronze Age enjoyed a good climate and there seems to have been an increase in population which was accompanied by a greater use of the gritstone moorlands. The presence of concentrations of scrapers, knives and arrowheads on the moors suggests that they were not just used for hunting but that occupation took place probably on a seasonal basis with herding of cattle. Horn cases of cattle are found fairly frequently on the moors. In Holme Clough four horns were found projecting out of a thick bank of eroded peat, and are now on display in Saddleworth Museum. Three of these are right sided, indicating at least three individuals. Bos horns have been found in other places on our local hills, including one not so far from the cairn at Rocher Moss, four near the site of Rocher Moss South Site 1, one on Round Hill, Stanedge, one on Millstone Edge and another on Worcock Hill. It has been customary to think of these horn cases as belonging to wild cattle (*Bos primigenius*), but Caroline Gregson examined the Holme Clough examples and thought that it was more likely that they were those of domestic cattle. Herding of cattle might have played a large part in forest clearance. Such activities may well have damaged the soil, resulting in erosion, podsolisation and eventually the spread of blanket peat.

It is possible that at all times the main settlements were in the valleys and it seems likely that by Late Bronze Age times this attempt to utilise the moorlands was failing. The Late Bronze Age material found in the Saddleworth area is nearly all in the valleys.

Trade routes have often been postulated and it is noticeable that there is a concentration of bronzes in the Aire Gap, and along the Yorkshire Calder to the Lancashire Calder, but T. G. Manby points out that the Aire Gap, forested and uncleared as it was would not be an easy route and considers that the stone and metal distribution 'rather illustrates the actual settlement areas within the region' (Manby, T.G., 1986) [23].

In summary, there is evidence for Bronze Age activity in Saddleworth throughout the Late New Stone Age to the Late Bronze Age and it is possible that farming (herding) activities on the moors in the Early Bronze Age may have contributed to the soil degradation and spread of blanket bog, with its impoverished vegetation that we see today.

CHAPTER 4

Iron Age

650 B.C. - 43 A.D.

The Iron Age in Britain dates from about 650 B.C. and is characterised by the use of iron for weapons and tools, but there is considerable continuity with the preceding Bronze Age in settlement, agriculture and crafts such as pottery. Some hill forts formerly considered to belong to the Iron Age have been shown to originate in the Bronze Age, and show a continuing tradition of fortification.

This is a period when the Continent exerted considerable influence over Britain, culminating in the Roman invasion of A.D. 43. Formerly, nearly all changes were ascribed to invasions from the Continent, but it is probable that most were the result of trade, social contact and indigenous development.

The climate, which had deteriorated in the Later Bronze Age, continued to be cool and wet in the earlier part of the Iron Age and perhaps for this reason this was a time of strife, as shown by the rapidly changing weapon styles and the building of fortified enclosures. Even today, more than a thousand hill forts still survive in Britain.

For the first time in Britain's prehistory settlement sites are common, ranging from hill forts and fortified farmsteads to unenclosed houses and hamlets. Considerable regional variation developed - some areas such as the Welsh Marches bristle with hill forts: others (including the Central Pennines) have very few, and this difference must reflect variations in social and economic structure.

Julius Caesar, discussing his invasions of Britain (53 B.C. and 54 B.C.), implies that whilst the inhabitants of Kent and the southern coastal areas grew corn and had a way of life that differed little from that of the Gauls, the inhabitants of the interior lived on milk and meat and were clothed in skins. Archaeology shows that this must have been a grossly exaggerated account but it may be that in the north there was a greater reliance on a pastoral economy. In spite of the poor climate, this is a time when the population increased, and a time when there was much forest clearance.

Air photography in some areas shows a landscape of fields, drove ways and habitations covering many square miles, particularly in the limestone areas such as upper Wharfedale and Upper Ribblesdale [89], and Riley, D. N. (ed.) *Yorkshire's Past from the Air.*

The older field systems have had later ones imposed upon them so that air photography provides a sort of palimpsest[12] so that it is particularly difficult to distinguish between Iron Age activities and those of the succeeding Romano-British period.

This is, of course, the age of the beautiful Celtic designs on metalwork, exemplified by the Battersea shield, and, towards the end of the age, the local inhabitants were emerging into the light of history and were recognisable as Celts, speaking a Celtic tongue and organised into tribes.

Illustration 36 - A recent photograph of the Mowroad Torc. 'Bronze beads of two different shapes strung alternately on a piece of iron of square section.' Found in 1823 beneath a flagstone at Mowroad Farm, Calder, north of Littleborough. (Photograph kindly provided by the Rochdale Museum Service). (1.5 times actual size)

The Iron Age in the Central Pennines

Occupation of the gritstone uplands appears to have been limited, and it is noticeable that on the western side of the Pennines such occupation as there was barely reached 650 feet (198 metres) O.D., whilst on the drier east side it attained 1000 feet (305 metres).

Pollen analysis from a number of localities suggests that, on the east side of the Pennines, there was a considerable reduction in forest cover at this time, perhaps in its inception as a result of pastoral activity, but soon accompanied by widespread cereal cultivation.

Bartley's work at Rishworth showed a great increase in the variety and quantity of non arboreal pollen types and a decrease in tree pollen values dated at 470 ±100 b.c. Bartley's evidence suggested that this process culminated in 30 ± 80 a.d. by which time a considerable amount of cereal growing was taking place nearby (Bartley, D. D., 1975) [21].

The story on the west is very different, with a remarkable absence of settlement sites comparable to those on the east, and it may be that the basic economy here was pastoralism although cultivation was not absent.

Barnes (1982) [1] points out that finds of Iron Age metalwork in the Central Pennines are very limited and that only six or seven pieces have been found in the whole of Lancashire, and some of these pieces were bronze.

This paucity may be largely due to the fact that iron work survives very badly compared to bronze work and pottery sherds.

Three of these pieces are reasonably local, one a small bronze ox-head ornament found in Manchester (Hallam, J. S.,) [61], another, a heavy beaded torque[13] necklace, found in 1823 beneath a flagstone at Mowroad Farm, Calder, north of Littleborough. This is in Rochdale Museum and is described in greater detail below (see Illustration 36).

An iron spearhead came from Blackstone Edge, just 300 yards south of the 'Roman Road'. This was very corroded and had traces of a wooden shaft in the socket. A fragment of an ox's horn was found alongside (Barnes, B., 1982, Appendix 2 - 158) [1]. This is also in Rochdale Museum.

The Mowroad torque is rather barbaric in appearance. It is 4" (100 mm) in diameter, and consists of 'bronze beads of two different shapes strung alternately on a piece of iron of square section'. The remaining segment consists of a bronze tube of rectangular cross section. The two halves are dowelled together with iron pins, fixing an iron tooth at each end which fits into an appropriate socket in the other half. Richmond describes it as 'a beaded native collar', comparing it with others in Northern England and Southern Scotland, and typical of the Brigantian area and very late Iron Age or Romano-British in date (Simpson, F. G. and Richmond, I. A., 1941) [25].

Two bronze harness rings were found on Stansfield Moor, which lies to the north of the Long Causeway between Todmorden and Burnley. These were originally in the Ilkley Museum but casts or electrotype reproductions are now in the Tolson Museum, Huddersfield.
Similar harness rings were found in the Honley hoard, Kirklees, (SE 13861241), but perhaps really belong to the Romano-British or Roman period as the hoard contained a Roman coin dated A.D. 73. It has been suggested that the hoard probably represents the personal wealth of a Brigantian tribesman including small silver coins of the Cornovii tribe.
Coritani or Corieltauvi

A shale armlet was found on Flint Hill, Rishworth Moor, in 1929 at a height of 1375 O.D. (Varley, W. J.) [90]. It is suggested that this is of Iron Age date, but a working area where shale bracelets and rings were being made was found on Totley Moor, near Sheffield, in 1959 which could be of Bronze Age date, and the Hunter Archaeological Society of Sheffield found over sixty pieces of worked shale at Swine Stye, on Big Moor, near Sheffield, which were apparently contemporary with this Early Bronze Age site (Beswick) [91].

Editor's footnotes:

12 A palimpsest is 'a piece of writing material or manuscript on which later writing has been written over the effaced original writing.' (Concise Oxford Dictionary.) It is used here in terms of the landscape.

13 'Torque' and 'Torc' are alternative spellings. Rochdale Museum describes the necklace as 'The Mowroad Torc'.

Pottery

Little distinctive pottery has come from the district. Details of pottery from Castle Hill, Almondbury, West Yorkshire, from excavations made between 1969 and 1972, are described by Gilks, J. A. in the Yorkshire Archaeological Society Journal, Vol. 64, 1992, pp. 17-23. [92] (see Illustration 37).

Some undistinguished pottery sherds came from Oldfield Hall, Meltham (see below), and the greater part of a late La Tène native pot found in 1958 in a natural cavity under large boulders in screes in Longdendale, (SK 055988) (Barnes 1982), App. 2, 84 [1]. When restored it made an almost complete vessel and is in Manchester Museum.

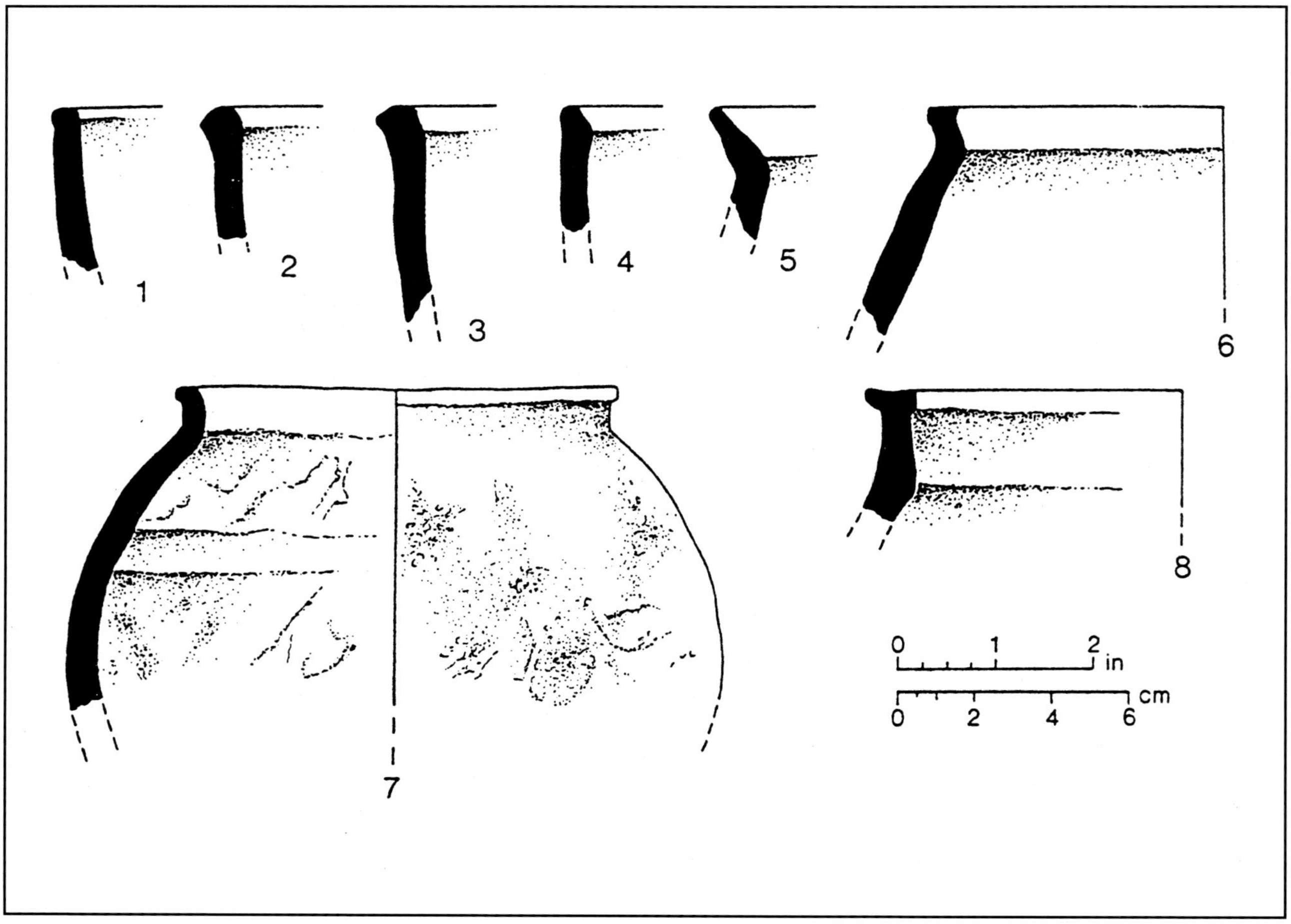

Illustration 37 - Iron Age pottery from Castle Hill, Almondbury. Scale: 1:2. (Reproduced from the Yorkshire Archaeological Journal, Vol 64, pp. 17-24, by kind permission of the author, J.A.Gilks and the Hon. Joint Editors of the Y.A.J.) .

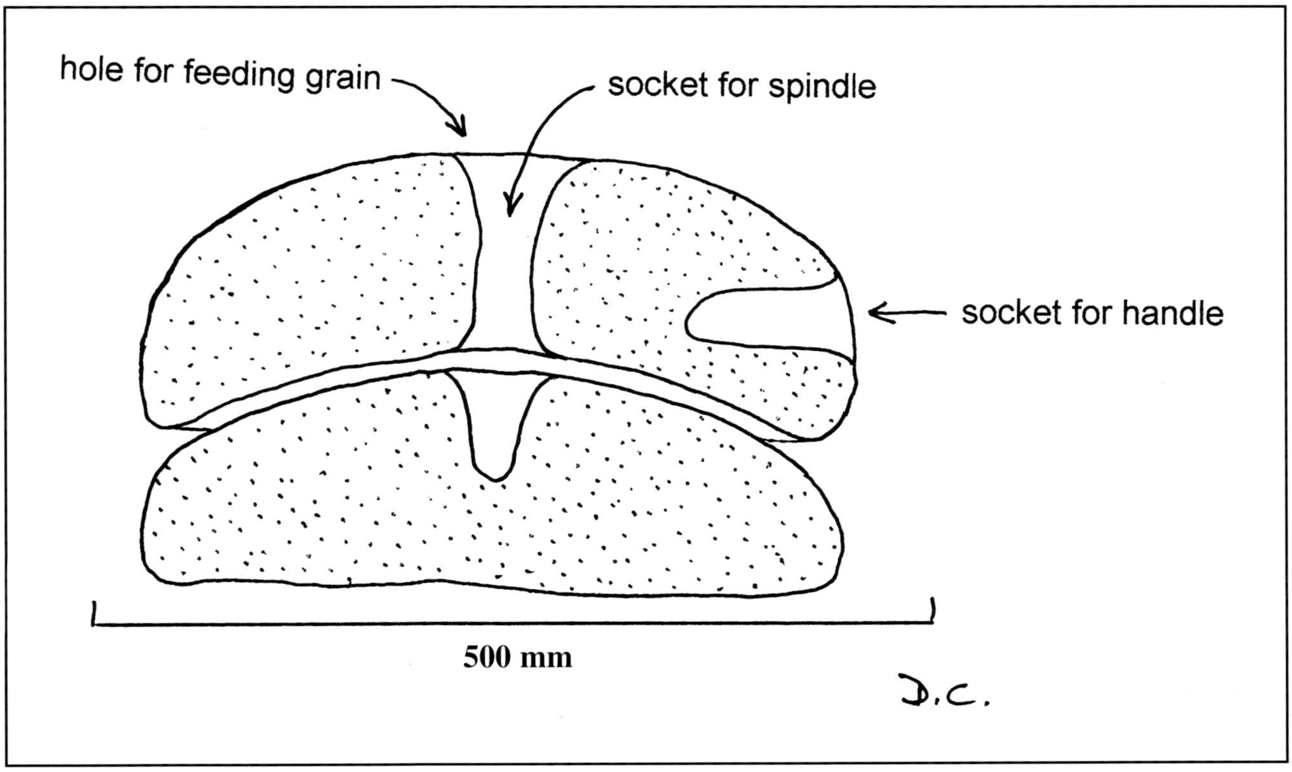

Illustration 38 - An Iron Age rotary stone quern. (Drawing: D. Chadderton).

Querns

Both Saddle and Rotary Querns were in use in the Iron Age, the Rotary type appearing in the later Iron Age. They afford positive proof of corn grinding. The majority of Rotary Querns come from the eastern side of the Pennines (there was a quern factory site at Wharncliffe, Stocksbridge, in the upper Don Valley) and two comparatively local sites where such querns have been found are Oldfield Hall and Royd Edge, two settlement enclosures situated near Meltham, which will be discussed below.

Earthworks

Locally, there are a number of 'earthworks' forming ovals and squares, not in Saddleworth itself, but in the neighbouring parishes. By far the most important of these is the hillfort at Castle Hill, Almondbury, near Huddersfield. This is situated on an outstanding 800 feet (244 metres) high isolated plateau which dominates the surrounding area.

Author's footnote:
Continental terms are used to describe the various British cultures - terms such as Halstatt, derived from a site in Austria; La Tène from another in Switzerland; and the Marnian after the Marne district of France.

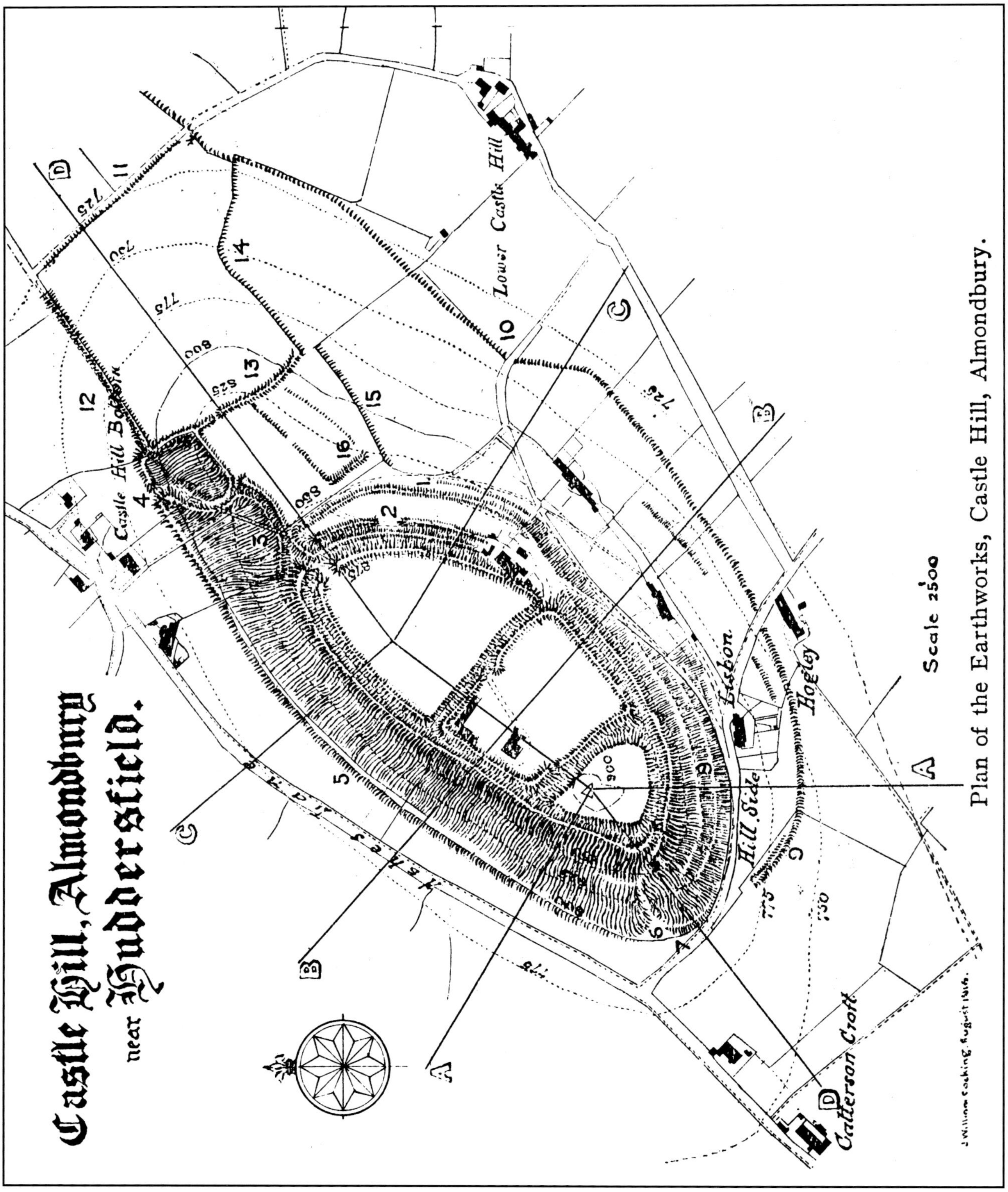

Illustration 39 - Castle Hill, Almondbury, Huddersfield. Plan of the Earthworks. (Reproduced from 'Early Man in the District of Huddersfield', by J. A. Petch, by kind permission of the Kirklees Community History Service at Tolson Memorial Museum, Huddersfield).

Castle Hill, Almondbury

SE 153141

Excavated by W.J.Varley between 1939-1972 [27], it has a very complicated history and a full excavation report has not yet been made. At some time before 2000 b.c. the site had a Neolithic occupation floor. Round about 600 b.c. the southern half of the plateau was enclosed by a single bank and ditch (a univallate enclosure). The site was then allowed to decay, but somewhat later some unenclosed circular stone-kerbed houses were built (Varley, 1976 [27] and 1973 [90]) (see Illustration 39 and Colour Plate 6).

Still later another univallate enclosure was made, roughly on the lines of the first one, and finally a much larger bivallate enclosure (two banks and two ditches) was made which contained the whole of the surface plateau. This was dated to 555 ±100 b.c. and covered eight acres. The fort apears to have been burned and destroyed around 500 b.c., its present appearance being largely the result of the Norman earthwork or castle built on the same site in the 12th century A.D. The fort was at one time considered to be one of the principal strongholds of the Brigantes, a confederation of Celtic tribes that controlled almost the whole of the North of England in Late Iron Age times - but if the hillfort came to an end about 500 b.c. this seems very unlikely, and certainly can have nothing to do with the dramatic story of the pro-Roman Queen, Cartimandua and her anti-Roman consort, Venutius.

This site is well worth visiting for the superb earthworks where the vitrified rampart is still visible and for the magnificent view from its summit, especially from the top of the 100 ft Jubilee tall tower built in 1897, a central place, dominating the eastern Pennine edge.

Buckton Castle, Mossley [14]

SD 98920161

Buckton Castle is a Scheduled Ancient Monument (Lancs. 7), standing on a steep-sided sandstone spur, at a height of 335m, overlooking the valleys of Carr Brook and the River Tame.

It consists of a single bank and ditch enclosing a roughly oval interior, some 45 m by 35 m in size, with its long axis aligned north-west to south-east. The interior is raised to a height of approximately 1.5 m above exterior ground level and is surrounded by a rampart which survives in places up to 1.5 m above the interior, and has an overall width of 2.0 - 2.5 m. It appears to be revetted internally and externally by unmortared ashlar blocks, fronting a rubble core. It is surrounded by a single ditch which is continuous to the south-west, where a natural slope renders it superfluous. Elsewhere it survives to a depth of approximately 6.0 m, and is up to 10.0 m wide at the lip.

Two entrances are visible today - to the south-east and north-west - but only the latter, which appears on 18th century plans, seems to be original. It consists of a causeway approximately 5.0 m wide, and 19th century reports state that a paved road led from it north-westwards towards Saddleworth.

Over the years a number of finds of prehistoric and later material have been produced from the area around Buckton Castle. Mesolithic and Early Bronze Age flint working sites are to be found in the immediate area, and in the 18th century, road widening operations along Moor Edge Road, beneath the Castle, revealed a necklace of gold beads, a broken silver vessel stamped with a crown and a silver 'duster' top - all clearly medieval in date.

The earthworks that can be seen today are those of a type of medieval castle known as a 'ringwork'. The possibility of its having been founded during the Iron Age, makes the site of crucial archaeological importance, since it would therefore represent one of the very few Highland Zone Hillforts in England, and one of the very few Iron Age sites in the entire West Pennine region. The Royal Commission on Historical Monuments describes it as a type of medieval castle, known as a ringwork of class B, superimposed on an Iron Age fort.

Buckton Castle is sited roughly equidistant between the Roman Forts of Castleshaw in the north and Melandra Castle (near Glossop) in the south, and lies very close to the alignment between the forts.

If Moor Edge Road is on the line of the Roman Road connecting Melandra to Castleshaw, and current investigations are producing evidence that this may be so, then it would be perfectly sited for signalling. From Buckton, the edge of Standedge above Castleshaw and War Hill above Melandra can be seen. Both sites are suspected signal stations. It may well be that a Roman Signal Station is buried between the Iron Age fort and the medieval castle: only excavation will reveal.

K. Booth & J. Cronin, 1987 [76] give a good account of the 'fort's' history, together with plans made by different antiquarians in the past. Other references are 'Buckton Castle', Tindall, A, Greater Manchester Archaeological Journal, June, 1981, and in *Land & Lordships in Tameside*, Nevell & Walker, 1998 [93].

Investigations have recently been started by the Greater Manchester Archaeological Unit which may throw more light on this enigmatic monument.

Editor's footnote:

[14] The sections on Buckton Castle, Oldfield Hall, Royd Edge, Highstones and Torside Castle were kindly contributed by Ken Booth, at Dr. Pat Stonehouse's request.

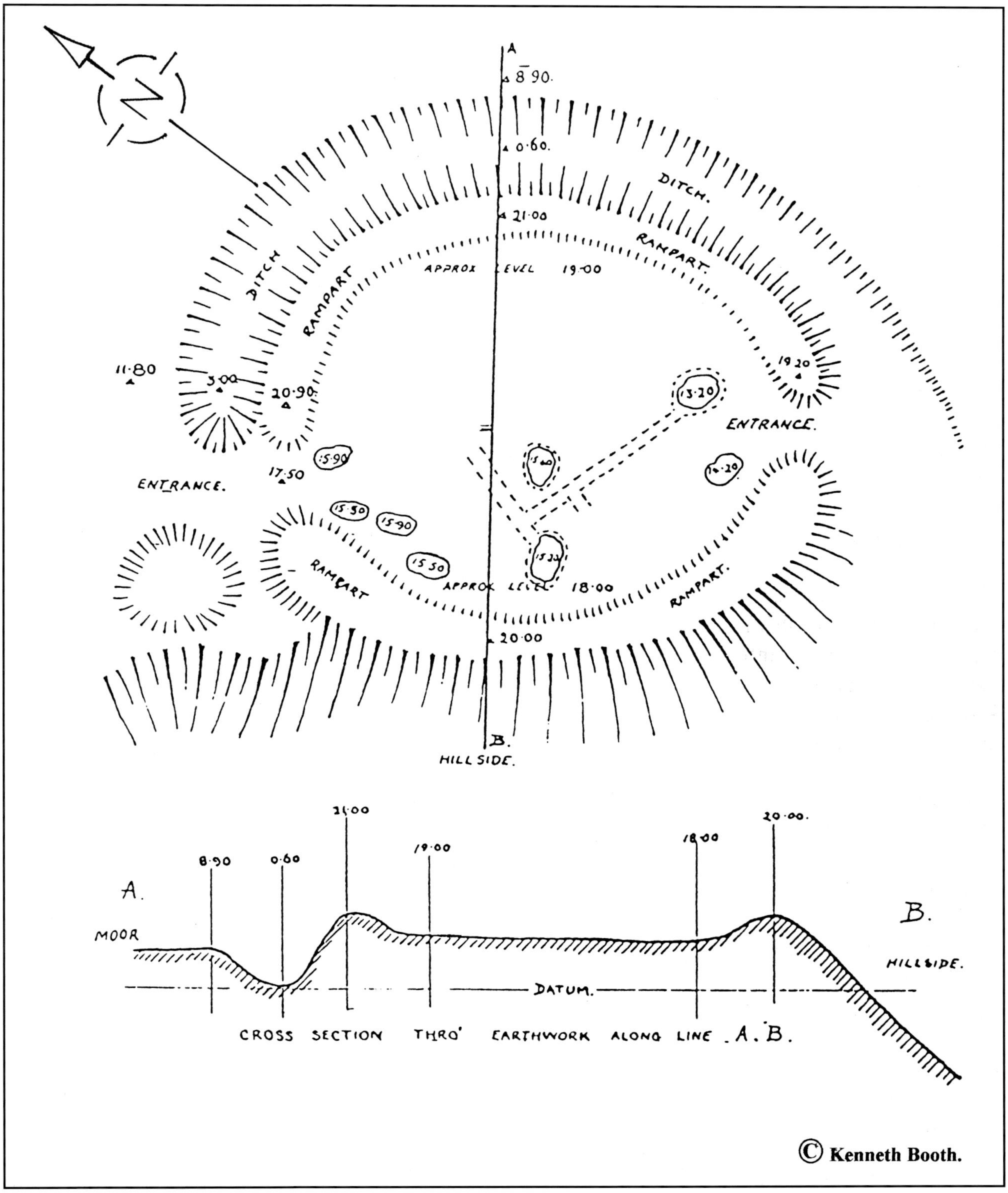

Illustration 40 - Plan of Buckton Castle, after the survey by Byram in 1941. (Drawing kindly provided by Kenneth Booth).

Oldfield Hall, Meltham
SE 0873 1010

On the slope west of Meltham is a D-shaped enclosure of about 1.5 acres surrounded by a rampart and a ditch which, in reasonable lighting conditions, can be seen on the right hand side of the road leading from Meltham towards Greenfield, at a height of c. 900 feet (274 m) O.D.

This is quite a striking monument whose revetted rampart may have been ten feet high and whose ditch was V shaped, five and a half feet deep and six feet wide, and cut into rock. The entrance, to the north-east, had a double timber gateway. The site must have persisted for some time as there was a pre-rampart palisade trench on at least two sides of the enclosure with vertical posts two feet across.

It was first excavated in 1923 when the ramparts and gateway were examined. The excavator considered that the remains were those of a Roman fortlet lying alongside a Roman road which came by way of Greenfield and Meltham on route to Castle Hill, Almondbury.

The finds included two stone discs, a rough cut rotary beehive quern, iron slag and some undistinguished pottery sherds. The quern showed that some arable farming was taking place here.

Subsequent investigations have disproved both Roman fortlet and road and have shown that Oldfield Hill to be of probable Iron Age date (Toomey, J. P.,1976) [29] (see Illustration 41).

Royd Edge, Meltham
SE 0910 0965

This is another 1.5 acre, semi-rectangular enclosure situated within half a mile to the south-east of Oldfield Hall. Excavation has shown that it had a stone-revetted bank, an internal ditch and an entrance in its eastern face. Aerial photography has revealed a possible circular building in one corner of the enclosure.

Finds include a fragment of a bee-hive quern, a leaden spindle whorl and flint chippings.

The fact that the earthwork has an internal ditch would suggest that it was a stock enclosure associated with Oldfield Hall which was the principal settlement (Toomey, J. P. 1962) [77].

Highstones, Tintwistle
SK 0643 9901

Discovered in 1978 and situated on a gently sloping south facing hillspur overlooking the Longdendale Valley are the well-preserved remains of a rectangular earthwork with rounded corners.

The earthwork measures approximately 67 m by 54 m between ditches which average 8m in width by 0.5 m to 1.5 m in depth. No evidence of a rampart or stonework has been found and the sloping interior is featureless but a causeway across the southern ditch would suggest a single entrance on this side.

Illustration 41 - Aerial Photograph of the Iron Age site at Oldfield Hall, Meltham. (By kind permission of the West Yorkshire Archaeological Service. See Reference [89], p.12).

The site is listed on the North Derbyshire Archaeological Trust record card as a possible Iron Age / Romano - British Settlement.

It has also been suggested that the remains could be those of a Roman fortlet or signal station serving an undiscovered Roman road passing from Melandra Roman fort, near Glossop, through the gap in the Pennines into Yorkshire. The site has yet to be excavated but quern stones of possible Roman date have been found in nearby field walls.

Torside Castle, Longdendale
SK 086966

This is a single banked enclosure, with no ditch, covering 3/4 acre at a height of over 1500 feet (457 metres) O.D. on a hillside on the west side of Torside Clough, which may be of Iron Age date (Preston, F. L., 1954) [78] (see Colour Plate 7).

However, the possibility has been raised that this may be a natural feature.

There are a number of other earthworks in the Huddersfield area that may be of Iron Age date, including the irregularly shaped enclosure at Kirklees Park, excavated by Sir George Armitage in

1906, but unpublished, and, like Oldfield Hall, considered by I. A. Richmond as a possible Roman fortlet (Huddersfield in Roman Times, I. A. Richmond, 1924) [31].

Sections of banks on Crosland Moor and Lees Hill (which overlooks the Roman fort at Slack) may also be of Iron Age date (Preston, F. L.) [78].

Discussion

The population was almost certainly increasing during the Iron Age, the paucity of metal and pottery finds being a very poor guide in this respect in this region and during this period. The inroads into the forest help to give a much better picture of what was happening. During the later Iron Age and after 400 B.C., the climate began to improve, the improvement continuing into the Roman period, when the population increased still further.

There seems to have been much more activity on the eastern side of the Pennine anticline than on the western so that a picture of a heavier reliance on pastoral farming on the wetter western side compares with a greater amount of arable farming on the east.

The presence of one of the largest Iron Age forts in the North of England at Castle Hill, Almondbury, suggests that the population in that area cannot have been negligible, but as recorded above, the Castle Hill fort appears to have been destroyed or at least ceased to be occupied sometime about 500 B.C.

From Saddleworth itself there is complete silence - no recognisable earthworks, field systems, metal work or pottery sherds, but a mainly pastoral economy would leave little remains, and this is true of much of the Central Pennines, especially to the west of the watershed.

North East Yorkshire, an area similar to Saddleworth with moorlands dissected by deep valleys, produced little evidence of Iron Age settlement until recently. Spratt, D. A., writes 'from being almost unknown thirty years ago, the Iron Age archaeology now shows the area to be heavily populated certainly in the latter part, and the first clearances and mixed farming to be at its most intensive' (Spratt D. A, 1993, *Prehistoric and Roman Archaeology of North East Yorkshire* (Revised Edition) London: CBA Research Report No. 87).

The story of Saddleworth does not end here - the local tribes must have come to terms with Rome, but away from the urban centres the farming methods must have changed very little.

It is, therefore, possible that further research has much to reveal in our area.

Addendum

Over recent years, since Dr. Pat Stonehouse wrote this section on the Iron Age, archaeologists have found a number of Iron Age sites in the West Pennines and Mersey Basin through aerial photographic analysis and trial excavation. This is beginning to change our understanding of Iron Age archaeology in the region, as Dr. Stonehouse rightly predicted above.

Norman Redhead, Assistant County Archaeologist, Greater Manchester Archaeological Unit, The University of Manchester.

Editor's note:
A detailed study of Saddleworth's Roman History is contained in the sister publication, 'Roman Saddleworth' by Ken Booth, published by Saddleworth Archaeological Trust, 2001.

APPENDIX 1

Francis Buckley

Illustration 42: Francis Buckley 1881-1949 (Photograph kindly provided by J.A. Gilks, Buckley archive).

Saddleworth's most famous archaeologist is certainly Francis Buckley - indeed his reputation in the 1920s and 1930s was both national and international and his work on the Mesolithic sites between Knowl Hill near Owd Betts to the north, and Longdendale to the south, probably did more to elucidate the problem of the Middle Stone Age in Britain than anything else and may indeed be regarded as fundamental. In the 1920s he re-excavated old sites, identified and excavated new ones, and carried out the most extensive field work in the Central Pennines that has ever been done. Moreover, he made notes and sketches about his finds, notes which are now preserved in the Tolson Memorial Museum, Huddersfield, where they serve as a treasure trove for modern workers.

He published some of his work in the Proceedings of the Prehistoric Society of East Anglia and other journals, and also privately. A list of his publications is given below. He was in touch with many of the most famous French and Belgian archaeologists, including the Abbé Breuil, who was perhaps France's most famous archaeologist at that time, as well as other well-known British archaeologists such as Miles C Burkett and Grahame Clark of Cambridge University.

The great importance of Buckley's work was that he identified two different flint industries in the Central Pennines which he named the Broad Blade industry and the Narrow Blade industry and he showed that all the Mesolithic sites could be assigned to one or the other of these.

With the aid of his French and Belgian associates he attempted to correlate these with continental industries such as the Azilian and the Tardenoisian, which led to some confusion so that he came to believe that the Broad Blade industry was younger than the Narrow Blade industry. This proved, eventually, to be entirely wrong, but nothing can rob Buckley of having been the first to recognise the existence of two distinct industries in the Central Pennines, which proved to be the key to a better understanding of the British Mesolithic.

Grahame Clark, who was later to become Disney Professor of Archaeology at the University of Cambridge, and Master of Peterhouse College, Cambridge, visited Buckley at his home at Tunstead House, Greenfield, prior to writing his definitive textbook, *The Mesolithic Age in Britain*, which was published in 1932 and accepted the validity of Buckley's two industries. However, Buckley's terminology remains in general use today, but Clark used the terms Non-Geometric and Geometric.

Illustratiom 43 - Francis Buckley collecting flints, probably on Warcock Hill, about 1920. (Photograph kindly provided by J.A. Gilks, Buckley archive, and reproduced with the permission of The Cambridge University Museum of Archaeology and Anthropology).

Buckley's standing as an archaeologist at this time can perhaps be illustrated by a quotation from the Abbé Breuil in his brief preface to Dorothy Garrod's book, *The Upper Palaeolithic Age in Britain*, published in 1926. The Abbé Breuil, after commenting on the comparative lack of progress in Britain in recent years goes on to write *'Depuis (since), des efforts nouveaux ont été realisé avec succes, soit dans les grottes des Mendips par la Société Spéléologique Bristol, soit par M. Francis Buckley dans les tourbières de Yorkshire, et j'ai salué tout ce renouveau avec joie'.*

Buckley had the habit of sending specimens for research from the same site to Museums scattered all over Britain and even to the continent - museums such as The British Museum: The Pitt-Rivers Museum in Oxford: The Museum of Ethnology and Archaeology at Cambridge: and literally dozens of others. Thus his material became split up, making the task of subsequent research much more difficult. This situation has, however, been largely resolved through research undertaken in recent years by John Gilks.

He also failed to locate some of his sites with great accuracy, and for this and other reasons he has been criticised by some (Hallam J. S. 1960) [61] but nevertheless his work marked a fundamental advance in Mesolithic studies.

He also realised the importance of environmental studies and co-operated with Dr T.W. Woodhead of Huddersfield Technical College and subsequently first Director of The Tolson Memorial Museum, supplying charcoal from his sites for microscopic identification of plants.

His publications on archaeological subjects include:

Finds of Flint Implements in the Red Line Trenches at Coigneux	*Proc.of the Prehistoric Society of East Anglia,* (1920-1), pp 1-9.
A Microlithic Industry, Marsden, Yorkshire	Privately printed, 1921 (Spottiswoode, Ballantyne & Co. Ltd.)
The Microlithic Industries of Northumberland	*Archaeologia Aeliana,* 4th Series, Vol 1, 1925, pp. 42-47.
Yorkshire Gravers	*Prehistoric Society of East Anglia,* Vol 3, Part IV, 1922, pp. 542-47.
Our Local Flints	*Oldham Chronicle,* Feb 24, Mar 3, Dec15,1923
A Microlithic Industry of the Pennine Chain Related to the Tardenois of Belgium.	Privately printed, 1924
Use of Pygmy Flints	*Antiquaries Journal* 4, 1924, pp. 47-48.
The Nature and Making of Graving Tools Found in the Huddersfield District	Appendix to *Early Man in the District of Huddersfield,* pp.87-92. Petch, J.A., Huddersfield, 1924.

It is worth noting that Petch's account of the Mesolithic in this publication is largely based on Buckley's work, and he writes that without his active aid this handbook could not have been written.

A man of wide interests, he was born on October 10, 1881, the second son of Arthur and Jane Buckley of Tunstead, Greenfield. He was educated at Wellington College, Berkshire and Trinity College, Oxford: qualified as a Batchelor in Civil Law: joined Gray's Inn on January 6th 1903 and was called to the Bar on November 17th 1905. He saw service during the 1914 - 1918 war with the 7th Northumberland Fusiliers: was mentioned in dispatches (see Illustration 44) and wrote an account of his war experiences published under the title: *Q6A and other places. Recollections of 1916, 1917 and 1918.* He also served as a Lieutenant, West Yorkshire Regiment, during the Second World War.

He was an outstanding authority on English Glass, and published a number of articles on English Glass, Old London Goldsmiths, and Old Lancashire Glass. He wrote what was to be the definitive work for many years on English glass entitled *A History of Old English Glass*, London, Beun, 1925. The greater part of his glass collection was donated to The Victoria and Albert Museum and the Tolson Memorial Museum.

He married in 1918, Bebba, youngest daughter of the late Dr Charles Clark Burman, who had been honorary doctor to the 7th Northumberland Fusiliers at the time of his joining the battalion.

The War of 1914-1918.

Northumberland Fusiliers

2nd Lt. F. Buckley, 7th Bn. (T.F.)

was mentioned in a Despatch from

Field Marshal Sir Douglas Haig, G.C.B., G.C.V.O., K.C.I.E.

dated 9th April 1917

for gallant and distinguished services in the Field.

I have it in command from the King to record His Majesty's high appreciation of the services rendered.

Winston S. Churchill

Secretary of State for War.

War Office
Whitehall, S.W.
1st March 1919.

Illustration 44 - The Certificate of the Despatch mentioning 2nd Lt. F. Buckley's gallant and distinguished services in the Field, signed by Winston S. Churchill. Reproduced by kind permission of J.A. Gilks, Buckley archive, and with the permission of Rosemary Pictor.

He became a J.P. and was a lay reader at St Mary's Church, Greenfield for many years, where there is a memorial window.

He died at Tunstead on the 27th March 1949.

W. P. B. Stonehouse (with additional information kindly provided by J. A. Gilks).

APPENDIX 2

Radiocarbon Dating

The following contribution was received from John A. Gilks, former Curator of Archaeology at the Tolson Memorial Museum, Huddersfield, following discussion with the editor about the radiocarbon dates given by Dr. Pat Stonehouse in the draft of this book.

The Calibration of Radiocarbon Dates

It was assumed by Prof. Willard F. Libby of Chicago, the pioneer of radiocarbon dating in the immediate post-war years, that carbon-14 forms and decays at a constant rate and that it has a determinable and consequently acceptable half-life.

However, we now know that his assumptions are incorrect and that the half-life of carbon-14, once thought to be 5568 years, is too low by as much as 3%; adjustments have to be made and the half-life is now set at 5730 years before present (present being taken as 1950).

Other factors have also to be taken into consideration; for example, different isotopes of carbon are absorbed by different organisms at different rates, whilst the level of cosmic radiation has varied throughout the centuries. These fluctuations have collectively made radiocarbon dates too young, especially before 1000 BC, by as much as 500 to 1000 years.

The problem of producing accurate (calendar) dates was only finally resolved by the discovery and subsequent dating of the tree-rings of the Bristlecone pine, a tree found in parts of the south-west of the USA, growing examples of which are up to 4000 years old, whilst dead, though still standing examples, and trees from peat bogs and river valley sediments in Europe, have extended the tree-ring dates back to around 10,000 years.

The outcome of this work has been the production of a calibration curve, a curve which must be used to convert raw "radiocarbon years" into calendar years BC.

The calibrated dates for the Mesolithic (Middle Stone Age) onwards, which are the periods covered in this book, are presented in table 3 below.

Table 3: Mesolithic to Iron Age Calibrated Dates

Earlier Mesolithic	c. 9500 to 6750 BC.
Later Mesolithic	c. 6750 to 4000 BC
Earlier Neolithic	c. 4000 to 3000/2900 BC
Later Neolithic	c. 3000/2900 to 2500/2200 BC
Earlier Bronze Age	c. 2600 to 1400 BC
Later Bronze Age	c. 1400 to 700 BC
Early Iron Age	c. 800/700 to 440/300 BC
Late Iron Age	c. 400/300 BC to AD 43/84

Further Reading

The following reading list may be of some use to those wishing to find out more about the periods discussed in this book, and in particular radiocarbon dating (especially in Greene, 1998), and the various methods employed in the recovery and interpretation of evidence.

Barton, N.	1997	*Stone Age Britain,* London: English Heritage/Batsford.
Greene, K.	1998	*Archaeology, An Introduction,* London: Routledge.
Hunter, J. & Ralston, I (eds.)	1999	*The Archaeology of Britain,* London: Routledge.
Malone, C.	2000	*Neolithic Britain,* Tempus.
Parker Pearson, M.	1993	*Bronze Age Britain,* London: English Heritage/Batsford.
Pollard, J.	1997	*Neolithic Britain,* Shire Publications.
Renfrew, C. & Bahn, P.	2000	*Archaeology: Theories, Methods and Practice,* London: Thames and Hudson.
Whymer, J.	1991	*Mesolithic Britain,* Shire Publications.

John A. Gilks, June 2001.

Saddleworth Radiocarbon Dates

The following is a letter sent to Norman Redhead, Assistant County Archaeologist, Greater Manchester Archaeological Unit, at the University of Manchester, from Professor V. R. Switsur, M.A., Ph.D., F.S.A., of the Radiocarbon Dating Research Group, Anglia University, Cambridge. This was in response to a request from Norman Redhead for his comments on the radiocarbon dates for local sites in Table 2 that are quoted by Dr. Pat Stonehouse near the end of Chapter 1 in this book.

Professor Switsur writes:-

'Dear Norman, June 18th 2001,

Saddleworth Radiocarbon Dates

The list of ages that you sent me were not written in the form that is currently accepted internationally but in the manner suggested by Glyn Daniel some three decades or more ago when there was some confusion regarding the use of two values for the half-life of the radiocarbon isotope. Willard Libby, the pioneer of radiocarbon dating, had obtained a value of around 5568 years whilst there was a new, believed correct, value of 5730 obtained by Olsson and others using mass spectrometry. These values differ by some 3% and so radiocarbon ages calculated from them also differed by this amount. Glyn suggested that we should, for the time being, use the notation b.c. for the radiocarbon ages but B.C. for what was believed to be calendar ages after they had been "corrected". Unfortunately multiple "correction" of certain ages has resulted in more difficulties. I will attempt to explain the present situation which has been arrived at by agreement at international radiocarbon conferences, which we hope will prevent further misinterpretation.

Essentially, the results obtained by calculations from radiocarbon measurements on samples are now designated as "*conventional Radiocarbon Ages*" and are given the symbol **BP**, there is now no use of "b.c." or "b.p." at all and there are no dots between the B and the P. The term "conventional" implies that a correction for isotopic fractionation has been applied and this is so in virtually all instances, including these Saddleworth samples. So when you include them in the report, please use the correct convention such as: Q-788, March Hill 2, 5850 ± 80 BP and include the reference in the journal *Radiocarbon* [Switsur, V. R. and West, R. G. (1975) *Radiocarbon*, **17**, (**1**), pp 35-51 {this also includes the dates for Radley's sites Dunford Bridge and Broomhead Moor}], and if there is space, it would be nice to include the reference to the conference in Los Angeles where these and other results were presented by Roger Jacobi and myself. (Switsur, V. R. and Jacobi, R. M. (1976) "A Radiocarbon Chronology for the Early Postglacial Stone Industries of England and Wales". In *Radiocarbon Dating - Proceedings of the Ninth International Conference, Los Angeles and La Jolla*, University of California Press, 1979, pp 41-68). This latter paper contains descriptions of flint assemblages for several Mesolithic ages and suggests a method, with examples, of estimating the ages of sites from their flint assemblages using cluster analysis, when charcoal is not available for radiocarbon measurements.

The radiocarbon age is always accompanied by its uncertainty term which is written with the symbol ±. It is sometimes stated that this is the "standard deviation" of the age, but this is incorrect. This number is, however, based on the one standard deviation *statistics of the measurements that go towards the calculations* of the age. Sometimes it is called the "error", again it is not, but is related to the statistical error of the measurements. In order to prevent confusion it has been recommended that the term "uncertainty" is used.

The isotopic fractionation (notation for this is $\delta^{13}C$ and is expressed in per mille, ‰) referred to above takes into account that the three isotopes of carbon ^{12}C, ^{13}C, and ^{14}C are not incorporated in the plants and animals in the same proportions as they occur in the atmosphere; there is a discrimination in favour of the lighter isotopes. If this fractionation is not measured and included in the calculation, the radiocarbon age may, in certain circumstances, be out by as much as 400 years.

It was the early work at Cambridge [Willis, E. H., Tauber, H. and Munnich, K. O. (1959) "Variations in the Atmospheric Radiocarbon Concentration over the Past 1300 Years", *Radiocarbon Supplement, American Journal of Science*, 1, 1-5] that alerted the community to the fact that the radiocarbon concentration in the atmosphere had fluctuated by more than 1% at different times. Their measurements were made on growth rings of known date from a Giant Redwood from California. The implication was that radiocarbon ages would not be correct since on Libby's theory, they assume a constant temporal atmospheric activity. Further work on the Bristlecone pine and other trees in different parts of the world indicated that these fluctuations occurred back as far at least as 7500 years. It was decided that a calibration curve based on measurements of dendrochronologically dated

Table 4: Radiocarbon Dates for local sites from Professor V. R. Switsur

Laboratory Reference	Conventional Radiocarbon Age BP	68% Probability Calibrated Date Range cal. BC	95% Probability Calibrated Date Range cal. BC	Dates from WPBS's Table 2 (on p.36)
(Rocher Moss South)				
Q-1190	5830 ± 120	4820 to 4540	4950 to 4450	3880 ±120 b.c.
(Lominot IV)				
Q-1189	5610 ± 120	4590 to 4330	4730 to 4230	3660 ±120 b.c.
(March Hill 2)				
Q- 788	5850 ± 80	4805 to 4660	4860 to 4525	3900 ± 80 b.c.
(Rishworth Drain 2)				
Q-1166	7550 ± 210	6560 to 6160	6780 to 5960	5600 ± 210 b.c.
(Dean Clough Site 1)				
Q-1299	7595 ± 140	6490 to 6220	6700 to 6100	5645 ± 140 b.c.
(Warcock Hill Site 3)				
Q- 789	8610 ± 110	7700 to 7500	7935 to 7480	6660 ± 110 b.c.
(Warcock Hill South)				
Q-1185	9210 ± 340	8660 to 7935	9070 to 7500	7260 ± 340 b.c.
(Waystone Edge)				
Q-1300	9396 ± 210	8660 to 8190	9010 to 8070	7446 ± 210 b.c.
(Lominot III)				
Q-1187	9560 ± 470	9180 to 8080	10,350 to 7840	7615 ± 470 b.c.

wood would be the best way of producing good calendar dates. The work by several dedicated laboratories on the radiocarbon calibration curve has continued during the past four decades and has been taken back beyond the Bristlecone pines range using Pinön and other pines and Douglas fir from America and more recently, with higher precision, oaks from Britain and Europe reaching back to around 11,000 years. (Calibration volume *Radiocarbon*, **35**, 1993). So we are now able to calibrate radiocarbon **ages** in order to convert them to calendar **date ranges** throughout this period. For ages greater than about 10,000 years the "uncertainty" after becomes increasingly asymmetrical and so the result is given as a range, such as 4805 - 4660, and in order to show that it has already been calibrated the notation cal.BP or cal.BC is employed, the latter indicating the normal Christian calendar. Beyond this period and back to about 30,000 years there is a calibration based on mass spectrometry of coral growth.

Unfortunately, because of the "meandering" of the calibration curve, there can be, and frequently are, multiple possibilities for the date range of a given conventional radiocarbon age. Some of these may be trivial but sometimes it is difficult to choose between them without other evidence. But this is another story.

Finally, it is usual to present the results of radiocarbon determinations at two different probabilities, corresponding to one and two standard deviations of the measurement statistics. Thus I present two calibrations here indicating that there is a 68% chance of the date of the sample lying within the one stated range or a 95% chance of it lying within the greater date range. These are given on the Christian calendar since most archaeologists seem to prefer this to the BP scale which suggests "years ago". This is rather odd since the people who inhabited the sites could not possibly have been Christians.

I hope these notes are of use in conjunction with the original tables of Dr. Stonehouse, whose sterling and meticulous efforts in establishing the archaeology of the region put us all in his debt.

With best wishes,

Roy Switsur.'

References: Switsur, V. R. and West, R. G. (1975), *Radiocarbon*, **17**, (**1**), pp 35-51, and reference [97], (Switsur & Jacobi, 1976).

BIBLIOGRAPHY (1)

All references are given as the author's name, initials and date of publication, followed by the reference to the book, article or other source. An alphabetical reference list of authors is shown in Bibliography (2).

The following abbreviations are used in the references:
Yorks. Arch. J.: Yorkshire Archaeological Journal
Brit. Arch. Reps: British Archaeological Reports
Proc. Prehist. Soc: Proceedings of the Prehistoric Society
Trans. Lancs. & Ches. Antiq. Soc: Transactions of the Lancashire and Cheshire Antiquarian Society.
Sadd. Hist. Soc. Bull: Saddleworth Historical Society Bulletin.
Arch. Ael: Archaeologia Aeliana.

1) B. Barnes 1982 *Man and the Changing Landscape*, Work Notes 3, Liverpool University.

2) Jacobi, R.M. Tallis, J.H. & Mellars, P.A. 1976 "The Southern Pennine Mesolithic and Ecological Record", *J. Arch. Science* 3, pp. 307-32

3) Thompson, F.H. 1974 "The Roman Fort at Castleshaw, Yorkshire, (West Riding), Excavations, 1957-64". *Trans. Lancs. & Ches. Antiq. Soc.*, 77, pp.1-13.

4) Clarke, D.L. 1970 *Beaker Pottery of Great Britain and Ireland*, (2 vols.), (Cambridge)

5) Poole, S. 1986 "A late Mesolithic and Early BA Site at Piethorne Brook, Milnrow", *The Greater Manchester Archaeological Journal* 2, pp. 11-30.

6) Gilks, J.A. 1976 "Excavations in a Cave on Raven Scar, Ingleton", *British Cave Research Assn. Trans.*, 3, no.2, pp. 95-99.

7) Gilks, J.A. 1977 "A Collared Urn and Pebble mace head of the early Bronze Age from Brown Hill, Saddleworth", *Yorks. Arch. J.*, 49, pp. 45-50.

8) Clarke, E.K. 1902 "Excavation at Pule Hill near Marsden", *Yorks. Arch. J.*, 16, pp. 8-42.

9) Manby, T.G. 1969 "Bronze Age pottery from Pule Hill, Marsden, West Riding, Yorkshire, and Footed Vessels of the Early Bronze Age from England", *Yorks. Arch. J.*, 62, pp. 273-282.

10) Wrigley, Ammon 1911 *Saddleworth - Its Prehistoric Remains*, (Oldham)

11) Bradbury, Joseph 1871 *Saddleworth Sketches*, (Oldham)

12) Bateman, Thomas 1861 *Ten Years Digging*, (London and Derby)

13) Hoskins, W.G. 1955 *The Making of the English Landscape*, (London)

14) Gibson, Alex 1986 *Neolithic and Early Bronze Age Pottery*, (Shire Archaeology)

15) Whitaker, J. 1771 *The History of Manchester*, (London)
1772 *The History of Manchester*, (2nd Edn.) 2 Vols. 13-15, fig 2, (London)

16) Cowling, E. 1946 *Rombald's Way: a Prehistory of Mid-Wharfedale*, (Otley)

17) Bradley, Richard 1978 *The Prehistoric Settlements of Britain*, (London)

18) Pierpoint, S. 1981 *Prehistoric Flintwork in Britain*, (Highworth)

19) Hart, C. & Spratt, D. A. 1985 "Gardoms Edge, Derbyshire, Settlements, Cornfield Hillfort", in *Upland Settlement in Britain*, (eds. D. and C. C. Burgess) pp. 71-76, *Brit. Arch. Reps.*, British Series 143, (Oxford)

20) Lunn, N. 1966 "Bronze Age man in the Pennines", *Huddersfield & District Arch. Soc. Bulletin*, 18, pp.11-15.

21) Bartley, D.D. 1975 "Pollen Analytical Evidence for Prehistoric Forest Clearance in the upland area west of Rishworth, West Yorkshire", *New Phytol.*, 74, pp 375-81.

22) Birks, H.J.B. 1965 "Pollen Analytical Investigations at Holcroft Moss, Lancashire, and Lindow Moss, Cheshire", *Journal of Ecology*, 53(2), pp. 299-314

23) Manby, T.G. 1986 "The Bronze Age in Western Yorkshire", in *Archaeology of the Pennines*, eds. Manby, T. G. and Turnbull, P., *Brit. Arch. Reps.*, British Series, 158, (Oxford) pp. 55-126.

24) Davey, P.J. & Forster, E 1975 *Bronze Age Metalwork from Lancashire and Cheshire*, Worknotes 1, Liverpool University.

25) Simpson, F.G, & Richmond, I. A. 1941 "The Roman Fort on Hadrian's Wall at Benwell", *Arch. Aeliana*, 4th series, 19, pp. 1-43.

26) Coombs, D.G. 1976 "Excavations at Mam Tor, Derbyshire", in *Hillforts: Later Prehistoric Earthworks in Britain and Ireland*, ed. D. W. Harding, (London)

27) Varley, W.J. 1976 "A Summary of the Excavations at Castle Hill, Almondbury, 1939-72", in *Hillforts: Later Prehistoric Works in Britain and Ireland*, ed. D. W. Harding pp.119-131, (London)

28) Aikin, J. 1795 *A Description of the Country from Thirty to Forty miles around Manchester*, (London)

29) Toomey, J.P. 1976 *An Iron Age Enclosure at Oldfield Hall, Meltham*, (Huddersfield)

30) Richmond, I. A. 1924 "Excavations at Meltham near Huddersfield", *Yorks. Arch. J.*, 27, pp. 319 - 320.

31) Richmond, I. A. 1925 *Huddersfield in Roman Times*, Tolson Memorial Museum Publication No. 4, (Huddersfield)

32) Watson, J. 1775 *History and Antiquities of the Parish of Halifax*, (London)

33) Spratt, D. A. 1982 "Prehistoric and Roman Archaeology of North-East Yorkshire", *Brit. Arch. Reps.*, British Series 104, (Oxford) p. 306.

34) Fowler, P.J. 1983 *The Farming of Prehistoric Britain*, Cambridge University Press.

35) Williams, Christine T. 1985 "Mesolithic Exploitation Patterns in the Central Pennines: A Polynological Study of Soyland Moor", *Brit. Arch. Reps*, British Series, 139.

36) Clark, J.G.D. 1932 *The Mesolithic Age in Britain*, (Cambridge)

37) Petch, James A. 1924 *Early Man in the District of Huddersfield*, Tolson Memorial Museum, Publication No. 3 (Huddersfield)

38) Buckley, F. 1924 *A Microlithic Industry of the Pennine Chain Related to the Tardenois of Belgium*, (Privately printed)

39) Clark, J.G.D. 1954 *Excavations at Star Carr*, (Cambridge)

40) Radley, J. & Mellars, P. A. 1964 "A Mesolithic Structure at Deepcar, Yorkshire", *Proc. of the Prehistoric Society*, 30, pp.1-24.

41) Stonehouse, W.P.B. 1980 "Rocher Moss South - Site 2 - A Later Mesolithic Site in Saddleworth", *Sadd. Hist. Soc. Bull.*, No.10, pp 21-24.

42) Radley, J. R., Tallis, J. H. & Switsur, V. R. 1974 "The Excavations of Three "Narrow Blade" Mesolithic Sites in the Southern Pennines", *Proc. of the Prehistoc. Soc.*, 40, pp.1-19

43) Albrethsen, S. E. & Petersen, E. B. 1976 "Excavation of a Mesolithic Cemetery at Vedbaek, Denmark", *Acta Archaeologia*, 47, (1976), pp.1-28.

44) Chaplin, R. R. 1975 "The Ecology and Behaviour of Deer in relation to their impact on the Environment of Prehistoric Britain", by A. E. Chaplin in *The Effect of Man on the Landscape in the Highland Zone*, eds. J. G. Evans, S. Limbrey and Henry Cleeve, 40-2. Counc.for Brit. Archaeol. Res. Reps. 11. (London.)

45) Mellars, P. A. 1975 "Ungulate populations, economic patterns, and the Mesolithic Landscape" in *The Effect of Man on the Landscape in the Highland Zone*, (see Ref. 44, above.)

46) Sahlins, M. 1974 *Stone Age Economics* (Tavistock Pubs. London)

47) Hicks, S.P. 1972 "The Impact on Man on the East Moor of Derbyshire from Mesolithic Times", *Archaeological Journal* 129, pp.1-21.

48) Dimbleby, Geoffrey 1978 *Plants and Archaeology* (London) p.150.

49) Gilks, J.A. 1973 "Bronze Age Pottery and a Basal-Looped Spearhead from West Yorkshire", *Yorks. Arch. J.*, 45, pp. 175-179.

50) Clarke, D.L. 1970 "The Beaker from Bee Low", *Antiq. Journal* 50, pp. 201-203.

51) Stonehouse, W.P.B. 1994 "Mesolithic Sites on the Pennine Watershed, Part II", *Archaeology North West, Journal of the CBA North West*, No. 8, (Vol 2, Part II), pp. 38-47.

52) Manby, T.G. 1974 "Grooved Ware Sites in Yorkshire and the North of England", *Brit. Arch. Reps.*, 9, p.98.

53) Davies, J. 1961 "A Polished Discoidal Flint Knife from Slatepit Moor, Lancashire", *Tr. Lancs. & Ches. Antiq. Soc.*,71, pp. 160-162.

54) Stonehouse, W.P.B. & Barnes, B. 1980 "The Medlock Flint Axe", *Sadd. Hist. Soc. Bull.*, 10, No 3, pp. 41-43.

55) Gilks, J. A. 1974 *A Neolithic Occupation Site at Castle Hill, Denby, near Huddersfield, Yorkshire*, West Yorkshire Metropolitan County Arch. Res. Committee.

56) Smith, I.F. 1974 "The Neolithic", in *British Prehistory, A New Outline*, ed. C. Renfrew, pp.100-136.

57) Stonehouse, W.P.B. 1978 "White Hassock; Prehistoric Arrowheads?" *Sadd. Hist. Soc. Bull.* 8, No.1, pp.1-3.

58) Watson, G.G. 1952 *Early Man in the Halifax District*, Halifax Scientific Society, (Halifax)

59) Barnes, B. 1982 "A note on Local Occurrences of Rhyolite", *Sadd. Hist. Soc. Bull.*, 12, No. 4, pp. 75-76.

60) Clarke, D.L. 1976 "Mesolithic Europe - The Economic Basis", in *Problems in Economic and Social Archaeology*, eds. G. de G. Sieverking, I. H. Longworth and K. E. Wilson, (London) pp. 449-481.

61) Hallam, J.S. 1960 "The Mesolithic of the Central Pennines", (unpublished M.A. thesis. Two Volumes. Liverpool University.)

62) Law, R & Horsfall, J 1882 "Discovery of Flint Implements on the Hills between Todmorden and Marsden", *Proc. Yorks. Geological Soc.*, 8, pp.1-15.

63) Law, R & Horsfall, J 1886-8 "An Account of Small Flint Implements found beneath Peat on Several Elevated Points of the Pennine Chain lying between Huddersfield and Oldham.", *Trans. Manchester Geol. Soc.* 19, pp. 599-603.

64) Stonehouse, W.P.B. 1986 "Dean Clough 1 - A Late Mesolithic Site in the Central Pennines", *Greater Manchester Arch. Journal*, 2, pp.1-11.

65) Young, Robert 1986 "Destruction; Preservation and Recovery in Weardale: A Case Study", in *Archaeology of the Pennines*, eds. T.G. Manby, P.Turnbull, B.A.R., British Series, 158, (Oxford) pp. 213-228.

66) Buckley, Francis 1923 "Our Local Flints", *Oldham Chronicle*, Dec 15th, 1923.

67) Stonehouse, W.P.B. 1992 "Two Early Mesolithic Sites in the Central Pennines", *Yorks. Arch. J.*, 64, pp. 1-15.

68) Jacobi, R. M. 1978 "Northern England in the eighth millenium b.c., an essay", In *The Early Post Glacial Settlement of Northern Europe. An Ecological Perspective*. ed. Paul Mellars, (London) pp. 295-232.

69) Mellars, P.A. 1976 "Fire Ecology, Animal Populations and Man: A Study of some Ecological Relationships in Prehistory", *Proc. Prehist. Soc.* 42, pp.15-45.

70) Coggins, T., Laurie, T. & Young, R. 1990 "The Late Palaeolithic and Mesolithic in the Yorkshire Dales" in *The Mesolithic in Europe*, ed. Clive Bonsall, reprinted in 1990. (Edinburgh) pp.164-174.

71) Larsson, L. 1985? "Late Mesolithic Settlements and Cemeteries at Skateholm, Southern Sweden". in *The Mesolithic in Europe*, ed. Clive Bonsall, reprinted in 1990. (Edinburgh) pp. 367-378.

72) Andrew, S. 1901 "Bronze Implement from Thornley, near Lees", *Trans. Lancs. & Ches. Antiq. Soc.* 19, p.240.

73) Green, H.S. 1980 "The Flint Arrowheads of the British Isles", *Briish Archaeol. Rep.* 75. (Oxford)

74) Stonehouse, W.P.B. 1987 "Mesolithic Sites in the Pennine Watershed", *Gtr. Manchester Arch. Journal*, Vol 3, pp. 5-18.

75) Andrew, S. 1892 "Bucton", *Trans. Lancs. & Ches. Antiq. Soc.*,10, pp. 46-66.

76) Booth, K. & Cronin, J 1987 "Buckton Castle, A survey of the Evidence", *Greater Manchester Arch. Journal* 3, pp. 61-66.

77) Toomey, J.P. 1962 "A Newly Discovered Earthwork at Royd Edge, Meltham", *Huddersfield & Dist. Arch. Soc. Bull*, 19, pp.1-8.

78) Preston, F.L. 1954 "The Hill Forts of the Peak", *Derbyshire Arch. and Nat. Hist. Soc.* Journal, 74, pp. 1-31.

79) Longbotham, A.T. 1932 "Prehistoric Remains in Barkisland", *Trans. Halifax Antiq. Soc.* pp.153 - 182.

80) Stonehouse W.P.B. 1997 "Pule Bents, A Possible Kill Site in the Central Pennines", *Yorks. Arch. J.*, 69, pp. 1-7.

81) Stonehouse, W.P.B. & Schofield, A. 1981 "A Late Neolithic "Burnisher" from Green Withens", *Sadd. Hist. Soc. Bull.* 11., No.4, p 82.

82) Clark, J.G.D. 1980 *Mesolithic Prelude*, (Edinburgh)

83) Stonehouse, W.P.B. 1982 "Gilbert's Island, the recent discovery of a possible Early Mesolithic Site, near Marsden", *Sadd. Hist. Soc. Bull.* 12, No.4, pp. 76-79.

84) Nevell, M. 1992 *A History and Archaeology of Tameside Before 1066.* Tameside Metropolitan Borough Council and Gtr. Manchester Archaeological Unit. (Chester)

85) Broomhead, C.E.N., Edwards, W., Wray, D. A. & Stephens, J. V. 1933 *The Geology of the Country around Holmfirth & Glossop*, Geological Survey of England & Wales, HMSO. (London)

86) Simmons, I. G. 1996 *The Environmental Impact of Later Mesolithic Cultures*, (Edinburgh)

87) T. W. Woodhead 1931 *Climate, Vegetation and Man in the Huddersfield District*, Tolson Memorial Museum Publication No. 8. (Huddersfield)

88) Brierley, J 1910 *Prehistoric Saddleworth*, Published privately by the Author. Hirst & Rennie, (Oldham)

89) Marriott, J. R & Yarwood, R. E. 1988 *The Aerial Time Machine, discovering West Yorkshire from the air*, The West Yorkshire Archaeological Service.

90) Varley, W. J. 1973 *Castle Hill, Almondbury, A Brief Guide to the Excavations*, 1939-72, Published privately by the Author, (Huddersfield)

91) Beswick, P. 1975 "Report of the Shale Industry at Swine Sty", *Trans. Hunter Arch. Soc.*, 10, pp. 207-211.

92) Gilks, J. A. 1992 "Early Iron Age Pottery from Castle Hill, Almondbury, West Yorkshire", *Yorks. Arch. J.*, 64, pp. 17-24.

93) Nevell, M. & Walker, J. 1998 *A History and Archaeology of Tameside, Land and Lordships in Tameside*, Tameside Metropolitan Borough Council and Gtr. Manchester Archaeological Unit. (Chester)

94) Stonehouse, W.P.B. 1976 "Red Ratcher, the Excavation of a Mesolithic Site in the Peak National Park". *Sadd. Hist. Soc. Bull.* 6, No. 2, pp.15 -22.

95) Stonehouse, W.P.B. 1982 "The Thomas Hill Collection (Saddleworth Museum)", *Sadd. Hist. Soc. Bull.*, 12, No.2, pp.34-36.

96)	Clough, T.H.McK., & Cummins, W.A.	198	*Stone Axe Studies*, Vol.2, CBA Research Report No. 67, pp. 210-217 and 219-221.
97)	Switsur, V.R. & Jacobi, R. M.	1976	"A Radiocarbon Chronology for the Early Postglacial Stone Industries of England and Wales", in *Radiocarbon Dating - Proceedings of the Ninth International Conference Los Angeles and La Jolla*, University of California Press, 1979, pp 41-68.

BIBLIOGRAPHY (2)

arranged alphabetically

A, B

Aiken, J. 28
Albrethson, S. E. & Petersen, E. B. 43
Andrew, S. 72, 75
Birks, H. J. B. 22
Bartley, D. D. 21
Barnes, B. 1, 54, 59
Bateman, Thomas 12
Beswick, P. 91
Booth, K. 76
Bradley, Joseph 11
Bradley, R. 17
Brierley, Joseph 88
Broomhead, C. E. N. *et al.* 85
Buckley, F. 38, 66

C

Clarke, D. L. 4, 50, 60
Clark, E. K. 8
Clark, J. G. D. 36, 39, 82
Chaplin, R. R. 44
Coggins,T. et al 70
Cowling, E. 16
Coombs, D. G. 26
Cronin, J. & Booth, K. 76
Clough, T. H. Mck. 96
Cummins, W. A. 96

D

Davey, P. J. & Forster, E. 24
Dimbleby, G. 48
Davies, J. 53

E, F, G, H

Forster, E. 24
Fowler, P. J. 34
Gilks, J. A. 6, 7, 49, 55, 92
Gibson, A. 14
Green, H. S. 73
Hallam, J. S. 61
Hart, C. 19
Hicks, S. P. 47
Horsefall, J. 62, 63
Hoskins, W. G. 13

I, J

Jacobi, R. M. 2, 68, 97

K, L

Larsson, L. 71
Laurie, T. 70
Law, R. & Horsfall, J. 62, 63
Longbotham, A. T. 79
Lunn, N. 20

M, N

Marriot, J. R. 89
Manby, T. G. 9, 23, 52
Mellars, P. A. 2, 40, 45, 69
Nevell, J. 84, 93

O, P

Petch, J. A. 37
Petersen, E. B. 43
Poole, S. 5
Pierpoint 18
Preston, F. L. 78

Q, R

Radley, J. & Mellars, P. A. 40
Radley J. R, Tallis, J. H. & Switsur, V. R. 42
Richmond, I. A. 25, 30, 31

S

Sahlins, Marshall, 46
Schofield, A. 81
Simmons, I. G. 86
Simpson, F. G. & Richmond, I. 25
Spratt, D. A. 19, 33
Stonehouse, W. P. B. 41, 51, 54, 57, 64, 67, 74, 80, 81, 83, 94, 95.
Stonehouse & Barnes 54
Smith, I. F. 56
Switsur, V. R. 42, 97

T

Thompson, F. H. 3
Toomey, J. P. 29, 77
Tallis, J. H. 2, 42

U, V, W

Varley, W. J. 27, 90
Walker, J. 93
Williams, Christine T. 35
Watson, J. 1775 32
Watson, G. G. 58
Whitaker, J. 15
Woodhead, T. G. 87
Wrigley, A. 10

X, Y, Z

Yarwood, R. E. 89
Young, R. 65